php|architect's Guide to Enterprise PHP Development

by Ivo Jansch

php|architect's Guide to Enterprise PHP Development

First Edition: June 2008
ISBN: **978-0-9738621-8-8**
Produced in Canada
Printed in the United States

Disclaimer

Although every effort has been made in the preparation of this book to ensure the accuracy of the information contained therein, this book is provided "as-is" and the publisher, the author(s), their distributors and retailers, as well as all affiliated, related or subsidiary parties take no responsibility for any inaccuracy and any and all damages caused, either directly or indirectly, by the use of such information. We have endeavoured to properly provide trademark information on all companies and products mentioned in the book by the appropriate use of capitals. However, we cannot guarantee the accuracy of such information.

Marco Tabini & Associates, The MTA logo, php|architect, the php|architect logo, NanoBook and the NanoBook logo are trademarks or registered trademarks of Marco Tabini & Associates, Inc.

Written by	Ivo Jansch
Technical Reviewers	Peter C. Verhage and Lorna Mitchell
Published by	Marco Tabini & Associates, Inc.
	28 Bombay Ave.
	Toronto, ON M3H 1B7
	Canada
	(416) 630-6202 / (877) 630-6202
	info@phparch.com / www.phparch.com
Publisher	Marco Tabini
Layout and Design	Arbi Arzoumani
Managing Editor	Elizabeth Naramore
Finance and Resource Management	Emanuela Corso

Contents

Acknowledgements

"Writing a book" has always been one of my "major todo items" in life. Next to learning to play guitar, running a company, getting a driver's license for a motorbike and appearing in the end credits of a major motion picture. (It can't hurt to set the bar high...)

I'm happy that the result of one of those items is in front of you.

For the past 8 years I have been involved with PHP; as a developer, project manager, system architect and finally as the CTO of Ibuildings, a European company dedicated to professional PHP services. It's only logical that the book would be about PHP.

During those 8 years I have learned a lot about PHP development projects. In this book, I'm trying to share this knowledge; I hope it's useful to developers and managers struggling with parts of the software development life cycle, and I hope it will help increase the quality of many professional PHP projects.

This book would not have been written without the help and support of many others. I would like to thank the following people who have contributed, directly or indirectly, to this book:

- Peter and Lorna; for the many hours they spent on reviewing the book.

- Elizabeth and Marco from php|architect; for publishing the book and supporting me during its creation.

- The Ibuildings crew; without them I would have nothing to write about.

- The PHP community; for creating PHP and getting it to where it is today.

- The people hanging around on the Dutch PHP channel on Freenode IRC; Andries, Eric, Felix, Mark, Michelangelo, Remi and Stefan, for inspiration and suggestions.

- Cal Evans; for inspiration and being a role model.

- My girlfriend Leoni; for putting up with someone who has spent the last 5 months in a word processor for 3 hours each evening.

- My parents; I would not be where I am today if it wasn't for the way they have raised me.

- And finally my late grandfather; it was he who introduced me to the wonders of math and physics and ignited my technology spark.

Foreword

We live in a fast-paced world. Looking over the last decade, the world has changed so radically - politically, economically and culturally - that it's difficult to believe only 10 years have passed. Technology is certainly no exception. It's easy to overlook the huge changes in the way technology is used in our daily lives - because technology tends to evolve in small little steps as opposed to one radical revolution. Looking backwards over a period of ten years provides a great perspective. The Internet has become so pervasive that the lives of many people today revolve around it throughout the day. They don't have to be computer geeks to spend hours and hours online - the Internet, in its various forms of consumption is simply their second nature - much like the phone was in the past. Even people who don't live their social lives on the Internet still use it as their medium of choice for performing many tasks - such as finding directions, buying goods, finding product descriptions or reading news. It is therefore quite obvious that the demand for Web-based solutions is booming with the possibilities truly being endless.

PHP was created in a brink of this new era, and while I can't say we knew exactly what was going to happen - I'm quite proud we took the right decisions that in turn made PHP one of the biggest enablers of this modern Web (r)evolution. I've heard many ideas from many people that tried to understand what is it about PHP that makes it so successful - its performance, excellent database support, support for protocols, its multi-platform support, and many other technical advantages. While there's truth to all of them, in my opinion they are minor contributors. I believe that there are just two key ingredients to PHP's success - Simplicity - being the technological advantage, and the Community that was built around it - that provided a huge social advantage.

Simplicity is the #1 technological advantage PHP has over its key competitors - it is simply the most productive option you have for creating and maintaining web sites; Unlike RAD tools, however - PHP's simplicity doesn't prevent you from building advanced and potentially complex systems. The Community, comprised of not only those who develop it, test it and document it - but also the millions who use it - has taken a life of its own, and is today a reason in itself for many to start (and continue) using PHP.

PHP's simplicity, while being a very positive thing, also created an unexpected negative side effect. It was so simple to use - that people without any background in computer science and no experience in development, could pick it up quickly and become 'dangerous' in a very short time. With the Internet becoming an ever more hostile environment, and with demand from users growing at exponential rates - it has become imperative for developers to invest more time in security considerations and proper architecture design. Ivo's "PHP in the Enterprise" presentation - comparing PHP to building blocks and modern applications to skyscrapers - is one of the best ways I've seen that illustrate this concept. This book doesn't concentrate on PHP itself, but rather on how you should use it if you want to build long lasting skyscrapers.

Happy PHPing!

Zeev Suraski - Founder and CTO, Zend Technologies

Introduction

This book is about PHP, but it is not about code. This may seem a contradiction, but writing software is not just about code. Every piece of software starts with an idea in someone's head and ends, not when the product is ready, but when the application is at the end of its life.

In the beginning, PHP applications were mostly personal websites, created by a single developer. It was not necessary to gather requirements or even to design the software, the code flowed directly from the developers head onto the server. Documentation would be overhead, as there's only one developer and he knows every part of the system by heart. For many applications, this methodology works fine. As PHP matures however, and finds its place in more complex applications and larger corporate environments, a need arises for a software process that is able to handle projects of hundreds of thousands of lines of codes, multiple developers, multiple server environments and high availability requirements.

This process, which we call the *Software Development Life Cycle*, contains many steps that influence the success of a project. This book tries to cover these steps, aiming to give you ideas on how to structure your development process, and to increase your productivity, or the productivity of your team. What makes this book PHP specific, you may ask? Many parts of the Software Development Life Cycle are independent of the programming language that is used, but each language has certain characteristics that need to be taken into account, and PHP is no exception. For instance, Object Oriented design in PHP differs completely from other languages, because PHP, by nature, destroys each object at the end of every page request. Another reason to target this book at PHP developers and their managers, is that the enormous increase of business critical web applications calls for a more standardized way of working; something which is fairly new for most PHP developers, given PHP's leniency and flexibility. In essence, the book maps best practices from generic software development, to the PHP world.

You may already use some of the things described in this book, or have heard a thing or two about them. I have structured the book in such a way that each chapter covers a different aspect of the software life cycle. So you may have a look at the table of contents and go directly to those chapters of the book that you find interesting, or you may read the entire book in its intended order. This is up to you. The important part is that you can use the book to improve your software development process. You may adapt the methodologies that I describe, you may adapt parts of them, or you may just use them as a source of inspiration to define your own software process, as each company and each project is different, and there is no "One Process" that fits them all.

Many topics covered in this book are so elaborate that entire books have been written about them. I will cover those topics just briefly enough to get you interested, or to get you started. Where possible, I provide suggestions for further reading.

I would love to get feedback on the subjects discussed in the book. Whether you agree or disagree with my views, I welcome any feedback. To provide feedback, please go to the book's companion website at http://www.enterprisephp.nl. On that website I will also provide errata to the book or other useful additional information that didn't make it into this edition.

Part I

Background

Chapter 1

From the Attic to the Cubicle

This chapter provides a short introduction into the history of PHP: how it started and how it has steadily grown into the language it is today.

PHP's Evolution

In the beginning, there was Rasmus.

PHP started out, in 1995, as a set of scripts, written in Perl by Rasmus Lerdorf, who was looking for a way to ease the development and maintenance of his online resume. When Rasmus had built an interesting set of tools (and had switched from Perl to C for development), he decided to release PHP to the public.

PHP was quickly adopted by many developers worldwide, who had found in PHP a language that was easy to install, easy to learn and very flexible. The official PHP website (`http://www.php.net`) reports that already in 1997, over 50,000 domains were running on PHP.

The Rise of Open Source

In the last years of the twentieth century, 'open source' software was rapidly becoming more popular. The basic idea is that the source code of software should be freely available. (If you would like to know exactly why open source is successful, Eric Raymond has written *The Cathedral and The Bazaar*[1] an interesting read and an important article describing the benefits of the open source development model).

For the Internet and its tools and applications, the open source model is successful because the Internet was growing at such a rate. In order to keep pace, development needed to be done in a way that development cycles ('time to market') were as short as possible, something which can be achieved for example by not reinventing wheels that others have already invented.

The open source movement spawned a number of applications that have contributed to PHP's success. First of all, to run a web application, you need a web server, and in 1995, the Apache web server was released to the public.

Then, there was the MySQL database. Originally released in 1996, it offered developers a database that wasn't as fully featured as the major databases of that time (Oracle, IBM DB2 etc.), but it was free, it was easy to learn and easy to install and maintain. There was a natural fit between MySQL and PHP, so PHP soon had built-in support to work with MySQL databases.

Both MySQL and PHP answered to a demand for faster development cycles of Internet applications. The Internet started to boom, and the traditional development tools just weren't up to the development pace that was required in the Internet revolution.

The LAMP Stack

The Apache web server, the PHP scripting language and the MySQL database engine were operating system independent, but around the time these products became popular, the free and open source operating system Linux was gaining popularity. The timing of these four products fueled the growth of each; the so-called 'LAMP' stack (Linux, Apache, MySQL and PHP) provided developers with an entire set of tools to run Internet sites and web applications. All you needed was some hardware and an Internet connection, and a set of freely available open source tools.

Most Linux distributors included Apache, MySQL and PHP by default in their distributions, which made installing a LAMP stack very easy.

---

[1]Information about *The Cathedral and The Bazaar* can be found at `http://www.catb.org/~esr/writings/cathedral-bazaar/`

Professional Adoption

PHP had started as Rasmus' personal project, and in the beginning PHP and MySQL were tools used by hobbyists for personal projects and personal websites. However, as the LAMP stack gained popularity, it quickly became interesting for professional users as well. As more and more businesses started to create Internet sites and web-applications, they too needed tools that allowed them to do so in an efficient manner, with a short time to market.

In the mean time, Zeev Suraski and Andi Gutmans (who would later found Zend) had joined the PHP project and completely rebuilt PHP into a more robust language that was ready for the demands of these professional users.

So it happened that within a few years since its initial release, PHP made its way into the cubicle.

The Maturity of the Internet

As the Internet grew, and after the bubble burst[2], the Internet became less frantic, more serious and more mature. Also, Internet sites became more dynamic and more interactive. People started to make money off the Internet, and e-commerce started to grow. 'Time to market' was no longer the only factor in web development. Reliability, security and performance of software became more important, and as Internet applications lived longer, maintainability was an issue as well.

This meant that the tools used for web development needed to grow, and over the years, both MySQL and PHP have had significant enhancements. MySQL started to feature transactions, views, stored procedures etc., and perhaps most notable in PHP, are the changes in object orientation. Object oriented development has significantly improved over the years, and in PHP5 it has become very powerful. Other changes over the years include the way errors are handled (true exception handling in PHP5) and support for major databases such as Oracle, MSSQL and DB2.

Ironically, both PHP and MySQL were in some way popular for not having all these fancy features, which made them easy to learn and easy to use. However, they have managed to add functionality as demand grew, while retaining the small learning curve and the 'keep it simple' mentality. Because of this, the LAMP stack can now

---

[2]See http://en.wikipedia.org/wiki/Dot-com_bubble for an extensive background of the 'dot-com bubble'.

rival the traditional and big commercial alternatives, but with a lot smaller learning curve, and a faster time to market.

For PHP, this trend also meant that its use extended far beyond the LAMP stack. Companies such as IBM and Microsoft worked with Zend to improve support for PHP on their operating systems, and PHP now plays well with all major database systems.

Web 2.0

The last few years, we have witnessed the rise of the so-called 'web 2.0 movement'. This movement is called "2.0" as it differentiates itself from the traditional Internet applications by being even more interactive, and allowing not only people to interact with websites, but also allowing websites to interact with each other. As the Internet continues to boom, and time to market is as important as ever, not reinventing the wheel has become even more important. Web 2.0 caters to this demand with so-called *mashups*; websites that are built entirely out of components or features from other websites. You can create an application that tracks packages from sender to receiver by combining applications such as Google Maps with the web services of companies like UPS, while writing only minimal amounts of code to glue the services together.

PHP has evolved with the emergence of web 2.0, by adding functionality to create and consume such web services, making it an ideal language to write mashups in.

This proves that PHP is in no way static. As the Internet evolves, PHP evolves with it, and continues to be a useful tool to create websites and applications.

Detailed History of PHP

In the previous paragraph I have tried to give a global overview of the evolution of PHP. If you are interested in a more detailed history of PHP, the differences between the major versions, the people that were responsible for developing it and a timeline, have a look at `http://www.php.net/history`.

If you are in a nostalgic mood, you might even want to try out older versions of PHP, which you can find in the 'PHP museum': `http://museum.php.net`.

Application Areas

In the beginning, PHP was mostly used to make websites more dynamic, for example by creating a CMS that allowed content managers or editors to change the content of their site. Nowadays, PHP can be found in a wide range of applications. Below is a list of examples where PHP can be found, some obvious, some perhaps less obvious.

- Websites
- Blogs
- ERP
- Wikis
- Intranets
- Extranets
- CRM
- Forums
- Accounting
- Logistics
- Middleware
- Bulk e-mail
- Galleries
- E-commerce
- HRM
- Project Management
- Tourism

- Government

- Healthcare

- Adult industry

Chapter 2

PHP in the Enterprise

PHP is entering the enterprise arena. In this chapter we will see some of the reasons why PHP is so popular that even big companies are taking it seriously now, and we will also look at the challenges that PHP faces. Finally, we will compare PHP to what else is out there.

PHP's Success Factors

PHP has had a steady growth from its inception and its growth still continues. There are a number of factors that fuel PHP's growth.

Built for the Web

First of all, PHP was built, from the start, for the web. It's main focus is web applications. Whatever you need when building a web application, PHP has a set of functions or an extension to meet your needs. To look at it another way, the features that PHP offers were created with the web in mind.

This means that when building web sites or web applications, choosing PHP will give you a toolbox that offers everything you need, directly built into the language.

Easy to Learn

Another success factor is that PHP is easy to learn. This means that the barrier for entry is low. Everybody who wants to create a website, can do so relatively easily by creating some simple scripts in PHP. You don't have to be a computer science graduate to be able to learn PHP.

This can however also be a disadvantage; we will get back to this factor later in this chapter.

Availability of Software

Because PHP is so popular, there is a lot of software written in PHP. Because of this, the language is very popular. For almost any type of website you plan to build, there is a PHP project that has written software for it: CMS systems, blogs, web-shops, forums, etc.

Widespread

PHP is a standard component of many operating systems. This means that at most hosting companies, PHP is available. Even cheap, shared hosting companies usually offer PHP. If you develop a web application in Ruby or Java, it can sometimes be difficult to find a hosting party. Because PHP is on so many Internet servers, that is never a problem.

Pragmatic

PHP has a pragmatic, no-nonsense approach. This means that it takes less lines of code to accomplish something in PHP, than in many other languages. PHP's function library is aimed at providing functionality for most common scenarios in web development. Working with arrays, dates, strings, regular expressions; PHP has many functions to be able to do most operations in a single line of code.

Time to Market

The final factor influencing PHP's popularity is 'time to market', or the speed of development. Although this is a direct result from several of the other points, I want to mention it separately, as this is an important factor.

The Internet is a fast-paced environment. If you have an idea today, you better launch something tomorrow, because the day after tomorrow somebody else will already have had the same idea and beat you to the market. So it's important to get something out the door quickly.

Another reason why time to market is important, is the difficulty to predict the response of the general public to an idea. During the first Internet bubble, many companies had marvelous ideas, and raised a lot of venture capital to realize their ideas. Then, after big investments and a year of development, they launched a site only to discover that the public wasn't really waiting for their invention, and they miserably failed. Nowadays, companies have realized that when they have an idea, it is important to get early feedback. This is one of the reasons why so many sites have an eternal 'beta' label. If you wait until the application is finished, somebody else will have beat you, or you might discover that nobody is open to your idea. So you apply the old open source motto 'release early and release often'.

Time to market is everything in the current Internet age, and PHP is focused on just this. Getting the job done quickly, and getting the job done right.

Enterprises that do not recognize the speed of the Internet often find themselves surrounded by small, agile Internet startups that rapidly consume a significant portion of the market. While traditional companies are struggling to find ways to bind customers to their brand names, companies such as Facebook that have no legacy at all rapidly create applications that attract an enormous amount of loyal users.

For traditional companies to succeed on the Internet, it is important to get rid of the old school of technologies, and to start using tools such as PHP that will help them create online opportunities much more quickly.

Enterprise Challenges

If we look at the above factors, many of them aren't really unique to PHP. For sure there are languages that are equally widespread, and there are other languages such as Ruby that might be considered even more pragmatic than PHP, but I believe it's the combination of the above factors that makes PHP so popular.

But, as PHP moves more and more into professional environments, it is also facing some challenges. While I'm a PHP evangelist, and talk to a lot of companies to convince them to use PHP, I encounter a lot of arguments why people hesitate to use PHP. It wouldn't be realistic to only mention PHP's success factors, so let's take a moment to address these challenges.

Easy to Learn, Difficult to Master

One of the advantages of PHP is that it is so easy to learn. One of the disadvantages however, is that PHP is so easy to learn. This is an apparent contradiction, but the problem with a language that is easy to learn is that it can be difficult to achieve quality results. If someone can create an application without much knowledge about true software engineering, the results can be dramatic.

This problem is apparent from many PHP software packages that are available; by looking at their code, it becomes painfully clear that many packages can not be considered secure, stable or scalable.

Another problem is that because of its flexibility, there are a lot of ways to solve a particular problem, and for many inexperienced programmers, there is no good way to tell if their solution is the best solution given the circumstances. It takes some trial and error before a programmer develops a solid set of best practices, so you can safely say that while PHP is easy to learn, it is more difficult to truly master the language.

If we compare this to a language such as Java, we notice that Java has a 'natural barrier'; programming Java takes a certain amount of programming skill, so it is not a language that anyone can easily learn. This means that, even though the best PHP programmers can compete with the best Java programmers, the least skilled Java developer is probably still a better programmer than the least skilled PHP developer. The range between high and low quality is simply bigger for PHP. This is one of the reasons why PHP sometimes has a negative image; PHP is for hobbyists and not to be taken seriously. But this is not the case; it simply means that you need to be careful what software you use and who you hire as a developer.

Companies like Zend raise the quality bar by introducing certification for PHP developers, so it is easier to assess the skills of a PHP developer, and more and more information is published on how to program in PHP with the right level of quality and a good set of best practices.

Inconsistency

An often heard argument against PHP is that the language is inconsistent, and to a certain extent, this is true. One of the inconsistencies is in the naming of functions and the order of parameters. For example, it is hard to understand why it's `str_pad()` (with an underscore) but `strlen()` (without an underscore), or why `array_search`'s parameters are `$needle, $haystack` while `strpos`'s parameters are `$haystack, $needle`.

But there are more inconsistencies. PHP5 has strong support for object oriented development, yet a lot of PHP functionality is just a set of functions instead of objects. PHP5 features exception handling, but many of PHP's internal functions never throw exceptions.

Luckily, tools such as IDEs with auto-completion help us out here, but I believe that as PHP adoption in the enterprise grows, we will see efforts to standardize PHP's syntax. It's a matter of someone stepping up and being responsible for maintaining consistency within the language. (Of course, backwards compatibility will be an issue to deal with, but it's not an impossible barrier.)

Persistent Objects

The HTTP protocol is stateless. This means that each requests is dealt with separately, and there is no standard way of maintaining an application's state across requests. Similarly, PHP is a stateless language. This means that the lifetime of objects and variables is never longer than a single request.

There are solutions such as PHP sessions to track data across requests, so an application can be made stateful, but this is still different from a persistent object that lives across requests and between users. If for example you would want to develop a high traffic game that multiple users need to be able to play against each other, you need an object that tracks the game state. In PHP, this can't be done easily. You would have to persist the game state in a database or memory cache, which, if the game is high traffic, is not always an option.

A strong point in PHP on the other hand is that it plays well with other languages. The above scenario would very well be possible by having a Java based service with a persistent state, combined with a PHP client that makes use of the service.

For most web sites and business applications however, persistence is not a requirement. If you need it, and want to combine PHP with a Java service, have a look at the following article from Bea Weblogic: PHP/Java bridge; `http://dev2dev.bea.com/pub/a/2007/02/php-java-bridge.html`.

Interpretation versus Compilation

The final challenge that PHP faces in the enterprise is the argument that PHP is an *interpreted* language which has some advantages, but also some disadvantages.

A compiled language is a language where the code that is written by the developer is first compiled to machine code, which can then be executed. An interpreted language however compiles the code at runtime, so there is no compilation required during development. One of the advantages of an interpreted language is that it saves time during development if you don't have to compile your code all the time. Applications are easy to change, as you don't have to recompile the code before you can run it.

There are however disadvantages as well; performance of an interpreted language is generally slower, since before the code runs, it needs to be compiled. Another disadvantage is that developers do not get "compile time errors" during development. If a developer forgets a semi-colon in a C++ application, he will notice directly when he compiles the code. So even before he runs the program, the compiler will tell him he made a mistake. In an interpreted language such as PHP, these errors may go unnoticed. They may only be encountered if during testing the faulty code is executed. If the code is not properly tested, it may even be rolled into production.

Luckily, these issues are solvable. In the tools chapter, we will look at development environments that can test the code before it is run, similar to a compiler. In the chapter on optimization we will look at "accelerators," which basically cache the compiled code so it doesn't have to be compiled all the time, and the performance penalty of being an interpreted language is negated. This way, with PHP we can have the benefits of an interpreted language, while not having the disadvantages.

PHP's Place in the Enterprise Market

With the advantages and challenges of PHP, where should we place PHP within the enterprise? For what type of application is PHP the right tool? Normally, we talk about "the right tool for the job." But since this is a book about PHP, let's turn that around.

The Right Job for the Tool

PHP is at its best in projects that involve the web. Internet sites, but also web applications. PHP can be used to build desktop applications using libraries such as PHP-GTK, but this has never become very popular. There are languages targeted specifically at desktop applications that are much more suitable for these type of projects. If a project involves a web interface, PHP is a good language to build that interface. However it's not just the interface; if a project involves web technology, for example a web service providing functionality to other systems, PHP is the right tool as well.

A type of web application that is gaining momentum is the business application. A business application is an application that is used within a company to solve an IT problem. This can be an order management system, a CRM system, a tool to manage data, a reporting environment, etc. In a distant past, these applications were standalone desktop applications. Later, when networks became popular and people started to share data, these became client-server applications, which usually consisted of a desktop application combined with a central database.

The past few years, these applications have moved to the browser. The obvious benefit is that the users only need a browser to access the application, which is a lot less hassle for an IT department. The application itself only needs to be maintained in one place, on the web server. These business applications, running in a web browser, do not have anything to do with web sites in the world wide web sense. However, the technology stack is exactly the same. It is this type of application where I see an enormous growth of PHP within the enterprise.

Once your internal software runs on PHP, and the external website runs on PHP, it suddenly is easy to integrate the two. PHP lends itself well to integrate business processes with the Internet. From self-service portals where clients can update their own data, to web shops that are fully integrated into the order management back office.

So basically, PHP's place in the enterprise is: anything that involves web technology.

PHP and Other Languages

We talked about the benefits of PHP, but there are more languages for web development, each with their own strong and weak points. How does PHP relate to these languages?

Ruby

Lately Ruby has been getting a lot of attention. Ruby is a 100% object oriented scripting language, with some powerful concepts not found in many other scripting languages. If you compare Ruby to PHP syntactically, Ruby has a cleaner syntax and is more powerful. Ruby, which has been around since 1993, has started gaining popularity when the Rails framework was developed. With this framework, it became easy to write web applications in Ruby. This has lead to a number of PHP frameworks emulating the Rails framework, some of which have gained popularity, such as the CakePHP framework. (We'll dive deeper into frameworks later in the book).

Ruby has a steeper learning curve than PHP, and the community is much smaller. This means that currently it's more difficult to get support, find third party products or even hosting for a Ruby application. It's interesting to note however that the PHP community tends to learn from Ruby and its frameworks, which makes PHP even more powerful: you get all the benefits of PHP, with the good things we learn from the Ruby community.

Python

PHP and Python are similar in many respects. This becomes evident when reading about it online, for example in the article *Python vs. PHP* (`http://wiki.w4py.org/python-vs-php.html`). In this article you will notice that some of the things that Python has but PHP doesn't, are already added in newer PHP versions, and vice versa. Choosing PHP or Python has a lot to do with taste. PHP has a bigger community though, so it's more accessible. Python on the other hand is used by some of the leaders in the industry, such as Google. This may have something to do with the fact that Python's creator, Guido van Rossum, is employed by Google. Yahoo for example, one of the other big players, standardized on PHP, but they employ Rasmus.

Java

Java is a general purpose language, but it can be used for web development as well; in its pure form, or as 'JSP' (Java Server Pages). An advantage of Java is that it has a natural 'barrier of entry': its learning curve is much steeper than that of PHP. This means that most people using Java know what they are doing, and quality in general is good.

On the other hand, PHP's focus on the web means that a lot of things you typically need when building a website are built natively in PHP. In Java, these either have to be coded, or third party libraries have to be used.

In general, PHP is faster in the development phase; Java, being a compiled language is faster at runtime. Despite this, PHP is easier to scale. While Java runs faster, it consumes more system resources, and scaling to multiple servers typically requires some architectural work. PHP environments are generally easy to scale because of its stateless nature.

.NET

The .NET family of languages (ASP.NET, C#, VB.NET etc.) all have their pros and cons. The biggest benefit of PHP over any of the .NET languages is platform independence. PHP runs on any of the major operating systems and many of the more obscure ones. While C# is a recognized standard, most of its libraries are only available on Microsoft operating systems. When choosing for .NET, you're really choosing a vendor along with it. PHP is open source, and not tied to any vendor or platform.

Zend is often considered the company behind the PHP language, and although they certainly support the language heavily and the company was founded by the two main architects of PHP, they have always ensured that PHP remained independent.

Perl

PHP has a history with Perl; the first version Rasmus created was written in Perl. This kind of characterizes the difference between the two. Instead of Rasmus building his website in Perl, he first wrote PHP in Perl, and then built his website in PHP. Perl is rather low level, and its syntax can be intimidating. It's a powerful language though, you can write pretty complex functionality in remarkably small amounts of code; the problem then is that this code is very hard to understand for a lot of people. In particular this perceived complexity is why many people select PHP to build web applications instead of Perl.

Other Languages

There are other languages than the ones mentioned in this chapter, but the ones covered here are the most common competitors of PHP. If you want to compare PHP to other languages, an online search for "PHP vs X" where "X" is the language you want to compare it to, is likely to yield several articles where the differences between the languages are explained. Keep in mind though that there's a lot of bias. Obviously, this book is biased towards PHP; similarly, sites focused on a certain language will be in favor of that language. For the best comparison, always read both sides of the story. Don't even trust this chapter, if you're really looking for a language to build your next project, properly research it. But since you're already reading this book, I'm confident that you already made that choice.

Hybrid Environments

One of the interesting things about PHP is that it is not mutually exclusive with other languages. I have already mentioned the PHP/Java bridge, which makes it possible to integrate Java code in PHP. There are also initiatives to run PHP code from within Java.

More and more, we see service architectures where monolithic systems are replaced by smaller components that run standalone but interact using web services.

In environments like these, through the use of standard protocols such as REST and SOAP, PHP can be combined with any of the other languages available. Later on in this book, when we talk about architecture, we will have a closer look at such Service Oriented Architectures (SOA).

Part II

Enterprise Development

Chapter 3

The Team

Development is about software, about code, tools, processes, but above all, it is about people. This chapter discusses the development team of a PHP software project.

Roles and Responsibilities

A development team may be just one person, or 42, but in any team a number of roles can be identified. In a small team, one person may have multiple roles, whereas in larger teams, it is more common to have dedicated roles. Regardless, identifying the roles in a team will help bring structure to the team, and will help create awareness of responsibilities; if, for example, nobody feels responsible for testing the software, bugs in the final release are inevitable.

   When reading through the roles described in this chapter, think of your development team (or if you are the entire development team all by yourself, think about yourself), and consider how the responsibilities described here are covered within your team.

The Customer

"That's odd," you might think. "The customer as a part of the development team?" It's really not that strange: the customer is as much a factor in the success of a project as any other member of your team. That's why it's important to have the customer actively participate in a project.

It's also important to understand who the customer actually is. I talk a lot about 'the customer,' not only in this chapter but throughout the book; some of you will be developing software for actual customers, but some of you will be developing software for yourself, or for your company. There is always a customer role, even in this case. The 'customer' in essence is the one that commissions the project, pays the bills, or defines the end result. Even if you don't have a literal 'customer' in your project, it is good to understand who has the customer role in your project. This can help avoid confusion. If you have multiple people telling you what features they need, make sure that someone is responsible for taking decisions when there are conflicting requirements.

The Analyst

The analyst is someone who is responsible for understanding the needs of the customer, and making sure that the solution being developed fits those needs. Typical activities of an analyst include requirements gathering, customer meetings and drafting functional specifications. Even if a project is too small to write a full-blown specification, understanding the customer's needs is an important job (so important that 'requirements gathering' has a chapter of its own in this book), as often the success of a development project depends on how close the developed solution is to the customer's expectations.

The Software Architect

The software architect's role is to translate the requirements, as defined by the analyst, into a technical solution. He may create a technical design, or just some rough sketches of how the system is going to be structured. In any case, it is the responsibility of the architect to think about the system before it is developed. If done right, during the design phase you will tackle all problems you will face when developing the solution.

Because of PHP's flexibility, there are often many ways to accomplish something. The architect of an application is the one who decides which way to go, based on the overall architecture he has chosen.

When development has started, it is the responsibility of the architect to keep an eye on the development, and see if it is still in line with the overall design.

The System Architect

Similar to the software architect, a system architect is responsible for thinking about the system before it is built. Where the software architect is responsible for the software, a system architect is responsible for the hardware. Many applications run entirely on a single server. Many others however run on clusters of servers, with dedicated database servers, web servers and load balancers. A system architect takes into account the performance and availability requirements, the number of users/visitors, etc. and based on this, designs an infrastructure of servers and a network.

The Developer

The actual development of an application is done by the developers of the team. But a developer has more responsibilities than just writing code. He is often responsible for keeping track of his own progress, and for informing the project manager of any problems he is facing. He is also the one implementing the ideas of the architect, and as such may have to discuss the (im)possibilities of the implementation with the architect.

Another important responsibility is documenting the code. While many developers seem to think that writing documentation is a role best performed by someone else, it is an important part of the developer's responsibility. Code documentation is intended to explain other developers those things that are not clear from reading the code itself. It should provide insight into why a piece of code is the way it is. Since the developer is the one who knows the thoughts behind the code, he is the perfect candidate to document it.

The Lead Developer

A lead developer has the same responsibilities as the other developers, but also has a few additional ones. A lead developer should coach the other developers, and help them solve problems they may face. This developer, who is usually the more experienced member of the team, will also be able to make sure the implementation closely follows the design, and no 'feature creep' will take place. The lead developer has a big influence on the quality of the code.

The (Graphic) Designer

"It's what's inside that counts."

As much as that is true, the perception of users depends very much on the look and feel of an application or website. No matter how good the application is, if the interface looks inconsistent, it will feel less robust.

It is important to recognize the role of designer in a project. It is good to have someone in charge of the overall layout of an application. This can go from completely designing the user interface (which is easier if layout and logic are separated using a template engine) to just defining some user interface guidelines that developers should stick to.

Even if the layout is determined by the developers, an important responsibility is to create layout consistency throughout the application.

The Tester

Testing is an important part in ensuring that software works the way it should. The role of 'tester' is often performed by developers for the technical aspect and by users for the functional aspect. One problem arising from having developers test their own code is that, no matter how good they are, they are influenced by the way their code was created. When testing it, they will take into account exactly those situations that they already took into account when writing the code. If you test someone else's code, you may think of scenarios that the other person didn't think of. So even if you do not have a dedicated test team, it is a good idea to have developers test each other's code, instead of their own.

The Project Manager

A project manager has many responsibilities. He is responsible for planning the project, keeping the project within budget, and solving problems. In short, he solves any problem that endangers project progress.

A lot of the project manager's tasks have to do with communication; communicating to the customer about project progress and communicating with all team members. Even in development projects that do not have a dedicated project manager, it is wise to assign the role of project manager to someone, so that it is clear who is responsible for running the project.

The Account Manager

If you develop projects for customers, your projects may benefit from the account manager role. An account manager cultivates the relationship with the customer. Although project management and account management are often done by the same person within a project, there are situations where it helps to split these roles. An account manager can keep a more independent relationship with the customer, and signal if the customer is unhappy with the way the project is run by the project manager.

By separating the account manager and project manager roles, there will also be less conflicts of interest. The project manager can concentrate on running the project to the best of his abilities, while the account manager can take care of recognizing commercial opportunities.

The System Administrator

The system that the application will be installed on is created by a system administrator. He builds the servers, installs the operating system, a web server, PHP, a database and any additional software that is required.

Even before a project is finished, a system administrator may have to build development environments and test environments. Later in the project, he will maintain the systems.

The Code Manager

Code is important and should be treated as such; it needs to be managed. If multiple developers are working together, the code they write should be integrated at some point, regardless of whether source control is being used.

Also, when finished, the project needs to be deployed. Deploying the project means taking the code and placing it on the server. While it is usually not a dedicated person handling this, it is an important role to identify.

The Trainer

When a project is complete, users may need to be trained, in particular if the project developed an application. It is unusual to train website users but there is often a back-end that administrators will need to be trained to use. The trainer should relate the solutions that have been created to the end-user. An important responsibility of the trainer is to explain how the application solves the customer's problem and, as such, he plays an important part in ensuring that the customer's expectations of the software are in line with what has been created.

Training

Things move fast on the Internet, so it's important to keep your knowledge up to date.

The importance of training is often underestimated. Managers see 2 problems with training: they cost money, and they cost time (and thus money). However, proper training can save money, because it helps people become more effective.

When I encounter managers that are wary of training, I usually give them a quick example calculation: if the team has 10 developers, and you want to grow the business by having 10% more work done, you can add an extra developer. This is expensive, costing a year's salary. Alternatively you can look at the existing team and see if you can make them 10% more productive. This means you have to train them and work on the parts that have room for improvement (trust me, there's always room for improvement). This can get you a 10% increase of productivity at a fraction of the cost of hiring an extra developer. In other words, proper training is worth more than it costs. However for this to work, you have to carefully select the training.

Below are some guidelines that can help you when considering training.

Training Requirements

There are many, many PHP courses available. The more popular a language becomes, the more training companies will want to convert that popularity into training courses. PHP courses can cover anything from the bare basics, to specialist or niche subjects.

In the years that I've been working with PHP developers, I've seen many different courses, and there are a few things I have learned and want to share with you. Developers need to be motivated and challenged by a training. There's nothing more frustrating than getting a 3 day training where the first 2 days consist of topics the trainee already knows. By the time the new materials are introduced, his motivation will have dropped so much that these topics will hardly be registered.

When selecting a training course, check if the topics discussed are close to the needs of your company. There are training institutes that offer onsite, customized training, that is tailored to the needs of the development team. This is usually more expensive than class-based training, but the quality is usually higher because the instructor can adjust the training to the needs and abilities of the development team.

Another thing to remember is that (in particular senior) developers are usually curious and want to know everything about a topic. I've seen trainers give a wonderful presentation, but as soon as the audience asked a question that went deeper than the slides, they were clueless. Many training companies, especially the ones that just pick popular topics and throw together a training, make the mistake of hiring trainers who predominantly have experience in giving slide based training.

With PHP however, it is much more valuable to work from actual experience. So, when selecting a training institute, pick one that knows PHP. One that employs PHP developers, or that employs trainers who have a history with PHP. Let senior developers review a training institute and their materials before deciding to send in all junior developers.

Finally, you learn PHP best by doing, so select a course that has exercises or that lets you work on a project. Slides are nice, but actual coding will be remembered much longer.

Certification

Red Hat Certified Technician, Certified MySQL Developer; there's a certification for almost anything you do as an engineer. There's a certification for PHP too, and it is issued by Zend. By completing the certification exam, you get the 'Zend Certified Engineer' (ZCE) title. There was a separate certification for PHP4; the current one covers PHP5 and it's likely that for any major PHP version there will be a separate certification.

There are several advantages to becoming a ZCE, both personal and for the company :

- It shows you take PHP seriously, and have reached a certain level of maturity in your PHP development. As an individual, this can help convince potential employers of your skills, and as a company, it can help you set yourself apart from the competition.

- Anybody who is a ZCE will be listed in the Zend 'yellow pages' at zend.com[1], including their company name. (There's also a ZCE logo you can use on websites and business cards)

- At some conferences you get some benefits (such as a 'ZCE dinner').

- It motivates developers if they can become certified, paid by their employer.

- To successfully pass the exam, you have to study a significant portion of PHP. Sure, your experience will be a major factor, but there are always topics that you don't encounter on a regular basis, but which are questioned during the exam. By studying for the exam, you will learn things that you didn't know existed in PHP, and it will also freshen up knowledge of features that you don't use often.

The ZCE exam isn't very expensive (at the time of writing, $125 for the exam and $33 for the study guide), so given the above benefits it is well worth it. For managers, there are a few things to consider when certifying developers or when hiring certified engineers:

---

[1] The Zend yellow pages can be found at: http://www.zend.com/store/education/certification/yellow-pages.php

- The certification is personal; this means that even if the company covers the cost of certification, when the ZCE leaves the company, he will take the certificate with him. So far, there isn't a 'Zend Certified Company' certification, so in order to be able to state that you're certified make sure that if people leave the company, you have others that are certified. This isn't really a reason not to get certified, but it's good to know about it so it doesn't bring you any surprises.

- The ZCE certificate does not guarantee that a certified developer is a good software engineer, so don't treat the ZCE that way during a recruitment process. It does however assess someone's PHP skills and is a testament that they take PHP seriously.

- The ZCE exam is not easy, so if you consider certification, make sure you prepare for it. I can recommend php|architect's *Zend PHP5 Certification Study Guide* by Davey Shafik and Ben Ramsey, the online test exams, and if you want to efficiently prepare for the exam, you might want to consider taking Zend's certification training. Here are some resources:

- Certification Study Guide[2]

- Online Practice Test[3]

- Certification Training[4]

- The ZCE exam[5]

The examination process itself is straightforward; you buy an exam voucher at the above URL, and using this voucher, you can schedule an exam at a Pearson-VUE test center in your neighborhood (there are over 3000 centers world wide, so there's always one nearby) at a date and time of your choosing. At the exam-center, you will be placed at a PC where you will have to answer 70 questions. At the end, you will immediately see if you passed the exam or not. If you passed, you will receive an

---

[2] http://phparch.com/c/books/id/0973862149

[3] http://www.zend.com/en/store/php-certification/online-practice-testing

[4] http://www.zend.com/en/services/training/course-catalog/certification

[5] http://www.zend.com/en/store/php-certification/exam-voucher

official certificate by mail. How many questions you have to get right in order to pass the exam is a well kept secret, but if you fail, you'll get an analysis of your results so you can see what areas to pay special attention to on your next attempt.

Self-Study

Many developers learn well from books or other sources. I'll cover some websites in a minute, but first I want to discuss books. Books are, from a business point of view, one of the most efficient ways to learn. You can digest a book at your own pace, and the price of a book is peanuts compared to training.

For development teams, it would be useful to have a policy regarding books. If developers want or need books, then there should be room to buy them. (But then again, if you're reading this book, it means you probably already have a good policy on books). Naturally it helps to look up a few reviews of a book to see if it's any good, before you order it. Also, many books nowadays come with a PDF version, which can be useful as a reference when you need to look something up. PDFs are better searchable than paper copies; on the other hand, paper copies are usually more comfortable to read.

Community

PHP has a big community of enthusiasts. They are an enormous source of knowledge. Many countries and major cities have local PHP user groups, and it is a good idea to join them. User groups organize meetings or workshops on a regular basis, which is a good way to share experiences and exchange knowledge.

There are also many websites with PHP information, forums for PHP developers and other useful sources of information. A list can be found here at `http://www.php.net/links.php`

There are a few websites I find particularly useful:

- Planet PHP: `http://www.planet-php.net`. This is an aggregation of many bloggers from the PHP community. Following this site (for example with an RSS reader) will give you access to many blog-posts about a wide range of subjects. Some bloggers post reviews, others post news, yet others post tutorials; there's something useful for everybody on Planet PHP.

- PHPDeveloper.org: `http://phpdeveloper.org`. This is the primary news site for the PHP community. Where Planet PHP is an automated aggregation of many blogs, phpdeveloper.org carries a hand-picked set of articles, and as such is a high quality source for PHP news.

- The official PHP website: `http://www.php.net`. The official website contains the official PHP manuals, which in turn contain many comments from developers that give useful additional information. It also features a list of upcoming events. It's also useful to keep track of the release notes for PHP versions here; reading the release notes will tell you about new features and new functions that might be useful.

Conferences

There are many conferences focused on PHP that are worth visiting. Even though you may sometimes have to travel, a conference is worth considering. PHP conferences usually contain one or more of the following items:

- Talks/presentations on PHP (or closely related subjects)

- Workshops/tutorial sessions

- Exhibition area for companies/products/projects

- Socializing with fellow PHP developers

Compared to a training, a conference is usually cheaper, but can be just as valuable. Contact with other PHP developers is very useful, as developers can share their knowledge. Workshops or tutorials are often full fledged training sessions of half a day or an entire day. The talks at a conference can be about a particular subject, provide best practices, teach how to use certain features, they can demonstrate new features of PHP or any of the many PHP projects and libraries.

The exhibition area is usually used for companies to present their products and services, or to recruit developers.

A few years ago, PHP conferences were so popular that there were all kinds of exotic conferences, for example in a tropical resort or on a cruise ship. In more recent years, conferences have become more serious and more professional, and this makes it easier to convince management that a conference is worth visiting. Perhaps the most notable conference is the Zend Conference (or "ZendCon" as it is commonly referred to), which is usually held in the fall. It is the largest in terms of visitor numbers, and focuses on professional use of PHP; this conference has a lot of very useful talks for PHP developers, and also for (project) managers. The ZendCon website can be found at `http://www.zendcon.com`.

Another well known conference is "php|tek", organized by *php|architect*, the publisher of this book. php|tek is usually at the end of spring. More information about it can be found at the php|tek website: `http://tek.phparch.com`.

Both php|tek and Zendcon are in the US. In Europe, there are some other major conferences. The International PHP Conference, `http://www.phpconference.com` happens twice a year, one in May, one in October or November, both in Germany. Despite its name many talks are in German, but they usually list the language of the talk in the schedule. A big advantage of the IPC is the sheer number of talks (there are usually 3 parallel tracks).

The London PHP Conference, `http://www.phpconference.co.uk` is usually in February. This is a conference organized by the PHPLondon user group. It grows every year and has a wide variety of topics.

The Dutch PHP Conference, `http://www.phpconference.nl` usually happens in June in Amsterdam. This one is completely in English and is also growing every year. I'm biased though; my employer organizes this one.

There are many other conferences, in the US, Canada, Europe and other continents. A list of upcoming conferences can be found at `http://www.php.net/conferences/`.

Recruitment

If you want to grow your team, you will need to recruit developers. What are good ways to find PHP developers? How do you know they provide what you are looking for? Let's have a look.

Defining Your Needs

Wanted: Senior PHP developer. 3 years of commercial PHP experience.

This is a typical job ad. But often, you don't need a PHP developer. You need a software engineer. A common quote I use is: "It's easier to teach PHP to a software engineer, than to teach software engineering to a PHP developer." After all, PHP is "just a language". But the process of developing software is so much more than just writing code that focusing on "PHP developers" might unnecessarily limit the number of applicants. Of course, someone who knows PHP can be productive very soon after you hire him, but you may have to teach him many software engineering skills. Someone with solid software engineering experience, who has done Java for a while, might need a few days to get used to PHP's syntax, but once he has mastered that, you'll have a very experienced developer.

The above depends completely on your needs of course. When you want to grow a team, make a list of skills you require. This might include PHP, it might include software engineering, but also look at what field someone is going to work in. Front-end development requires different skills than database development, and creating a SOA architecture (don't worry if that doesn't ring a bell, I'll cover it in the chapter on architecture) requires a different skill set from that needed to implement a standard CMS.

Reaching PHP Developers

When looking for PHP developers, there are a number of things you can do to find them. The traditional way of posting a job offer in a newspaper isn't very effective, as many PHP developers aren't likely to read paper versions of newspapers. It's probably more efficient to post an advert on websites that are frequented by PHP developers, such as `http://www.phpdeveloper.org` or `http://www.planet-php.net`. The latter is a blog aggregator, which means you'd have to get your job offer mentioned in a blog that is syndicated on Planet PHP, but at PHPDeveloper you can directly post a job offer.

Also check the web sites of local PHP user groups and communities as they are likely to be frequently visited by PHP developers from your area. A relatively new way of recruiting is using social networks such as LinkedIn (`http://www.linkedin.com`). Many PHP developers have a Linked-In account. You can search your LinkedIn network for the keyword 'php', but remember that in the previous paragraph I talked about not only looking at PHP developers, but also at software engineers. You can search for both on LinkedIn.

Use online job sites such as `http://www.monsterboard.com`. Studies have shown that developers are using the internet as the number one source when looking for a new job. Both sites like LinkedIn and sites like Monsterboard are gradually taking the place of recruitment agencies. If you use a recruitment agency, make sure it's one that has an added value over these online resources. If they just collect and send out CVs, you're better off doing your own recruitment. If they however assess developers and help in the selection process, they might be worth the extra money.

Use your network. You may know PHP developers, or your coworkers may know PHP developers. This can be a valuable source for candidates. To stimulate people to recruit their friends, offer them a bonus if their friend is offered a job. It's often more effective to offer $1000 to individuals than to have to pay a lot more to a recruitment agency.

Assessing Skills

Assessing someone's skills in an interview can be hard. The general advice is rather obvious, and that is to try to see how closely a candidate matches your requirements. It is important to check communication skills in addition to technical knowledge; try to investigate software engineering skills in preference to focusing heavily on PHP.

Often the interviews are done by managers; it might be useful however to have developers participate in the interviews. After all, they have the technical knowledge to be able to assess a new developer, and also you can see if there's a match between the candidate and his future coworkers.

Here are a few things you might find relevant for an interview:

- Check basic PHP skills

- Check advanced PHP skills

- Check software engineering skills

- Check Object Oriented development skills

- Check experience with tools

- Have them analyze a problem. The solution isn't important, but have them think out loud so you can see how they tackle a problem.

Construct a code sample and have them analyze what, in general, is wrong with the code. For example, write some code that doesn't adhere to coding standards, contains a few parse errors, doesn't contain documentation, mixes HTML with business logic; in other words code that violates things that are covered by the topics in this book. Check what areas they investigate. Do they only uncover the parse errors or do they have affinity with analyzing the way the code was built? Check their experience and determine its relevance. Often, I encounter developers who call themselves 'senior developer' because they have been developing for 7 years. However, if they have developed the same, less-than-ideal, way for all those years, without actually improving their skills, they aren't really senior.

- Check database skills; often these are just as important as PHP skills.

There are many things you can cover; the above list is far from complete. But you might find this list useful as a starting point, and add your own specific checks to the process.

Being an Attractive Employer

Everybody is looking for PHP developers. So how do you make sure that people will want to work for you? (If you're a developer reading this, and are already recruited, show this to your boss; it might just make your own job more appealing.)

Developers are a typical group of people. A good salary is one thing, but there's more to life than salary. If we were in it for the money, we would probably have pursued a Java job. So although it is very important that salaries are right, I won't cover that here.

Here are a few things I, as a PHP developer, have found attractive at companies I have encountered over the years.

- Challenges make sure the work is challenging, so people can learn. Assign the right job to the right people. While for some people it may seem 'easy money' if you have a job that requires only routine tasks, for most PHP developers this will be boring and will make them feel very uncomfortable.

- 'Work hard, play hard'; Geeks like to play. At my company, people play street soccer (at least the more physically active ones; the rest play Unreal Tournament) during lunch breaks, do all kinds of activities (movies, bowling, etc.) and have many office gadgets to play with during office hours. Often, the teams that seem the most 'loose' and informal get the most complex assignments done. A company that encourages both work-related and non-work related activities, provides a stimulating environment for PHP developers. There are companies that have very strict policies about what is allowed at work and what isn't. Some companies even filter out certain websites because they don't want their developers to 'play around' at work. Trust your developers to be able to make their own judgement on how they spend their time, and measure them based on the results. Most developers do not have a nine to five mentality, and do not mind to do overtime, answer the phone when they are not at work, or finish that demo for tomorrow until 11pm. Flexibility works both ways.

- Fun rewards. PHP developers are often more motivated by nice, fancy or geeky gadgets than by rewards in money. While it may be stimulating to give a 100 dollar bonus once a year to every team member, that game console in the lunch room is probably a lot more motivating.

- Benefits. A laptop, internet connection, a phone are things that are not expensive for a company, but are very valuable to developers. If 'everything is taken care of', developers will notice that the company cares for their well-being, inside and outside of the office.

- Creativity. While this is closely related to the 'challenges' bullet above, I would like to stress that developing is a creative process, and developers should be able to express that creativity. Have developers create their own solutions instead of using them as 'code monkeys'. Often seniors tell juniors what to do and how to do it. It's much more motivating however to let them create their own solution, with help from the senior.

- Feedback. Talk to the developers on a regular basis and check how they feel about their work. Many developers are rather introvert and if they think something is wrong, they may not always talk about it. By actively talking to the development team periodically and provide them with a way to give feedback, you will create a development team that is able to improve itself and its environment.

Chapter 4

Requirements Gathering

Some customers are very good at expressing their wishes. Some may even provide you with detailed specifications. Often however, the requirements are much more vague. Think about it this way: what a customer expects is not always the same as what a customer asks. It is the analyst's task to not only uncover what the customer really needs, but also to bring the proposed solutions in line with the customer's expectations. In this chapter, we will look at the things you need to take into account when gathering requirements. (As in the rest of the book, when I say 'customer', I mean not only an external customer, but also an internal customer, in the case you're developing software for your organization.)

Business Goals

Before we start to think about requirements, we first need to think about the business goals. Why are we building a new application? What is our goal with a new web site? Often, this step is skipped, and requirements are gathered without realizing what the underlying goals are. Here are some business goals that you might encounter:

- Generate revenue: for example in the case of e-commerce, the business goal of building a web-shop will be to generate revenue. This is also the case for web sites that are driven by ad revenue.

- Reduce costs: self-service portals are an example of systems that help reduce administrative load, and business process applications are another example.

- Improve service: sometimes web sites are built not to reduce operational costs, but to improve the service-level to customers. Modern customers are accustomed to managing their own information and their own accounts online.

- Marketing: when the Internet was growing up, there was a time when web sites were nothing more than digital brochures. While there is more interactivity nowadays, web sites are often still a marketing instrument, trying to reach (potential) customers and offering services.

These are just examples, there are many more business goals. The benefit of knowing the goals of an application is that you can use this to steer development. When in doubt, or when you have to make a choice between several potential options, you can weigh your choices against the business goals and choose the one that helps the business goal.

If you know the goals, you can also help provide solutions to the problems that the customer is facing. In general, when a customer asks you to build a web site or application for them, there are two major groups. Some customers think in problems. They present you with their challenges, and leave it up to you to design a solution that solves their problem. Other customers think in solutions; they have already thought about their problems, and also know what the solution is. This type of customer often provides detailed specifications or even a functional requirements document.

There are advantages and disadvantages to both approaches. In the first case, the disadvantage is that the requirements are usually more vague, and it will take longer to design a solution. In the second case, your opinion regarding solutions may differ from the customer's. On the other hand, the advantage of the first case is that it allows for greater creativity, whereas the second will give you a well-defined set of requirements and make it easier to satisfy the customer. Also, the customer has the best knowledge of his field, so it's very useful if he has already thought of solutions.

Even if the customer already provides the solution, it is a good thing to ask about the problems they are trying to solve. This helps steer your decisions, and if there's a difference of opinion regarding certain functionality, knowing what problem they are trying to solve will help you get to the right solution.

A risk that I have encountered on many occasions is the situation where the customer appears to present his problems to you, but already has a solution in mind. In this case, it's hard to manage expectations. It is a good thing to talk about this. If your customer describes the problem he is trying to solve, ask him if he has already given thought to the solution.

Equally dangerous is the situation where the customer gives you the requirements to an application, but along the way you find out that the customer has not thought about the problems he is trying to solve, and as such, the solution, even if he designed it himself, will not solve his problems. Again, talking to the customer and discovering his motivations will help to avoid problems during the course of the project.

Expectation Management

Once you know the goals, it's time to start defining the requirements. There are three main reasons you need to document the requirements:

- The development team needs to know what they are going to build.

- If you know what you are going to build, you can estimate what it is going to cost and how long it will take.

- The customer needs to know what he's going to get.

This last bullet is important, as it helps you to manage the expectations of the customer. If you're not building what the client expects you to build, the client is going to be disappointed. Since there's always room for misinterpretations, it helps to document the requirements, so the customer can verify if you understood his wishes.

The greater the level of detail in the requirements, the closer the end result will be to the expectations of the client. Sometimes, requirements are documented overly formally and almost mathematical. While this helps in the case of legal issues to defend a solution against a complaining customer, it's almost always better to make the requirements easy to understand. This will make it easier for the customer to see what you are going to build, and easier for the developers to know what is expected of them. This can keep you out of legal issues in the first place.

Functional Requirements

When documenting the requirements, it is good practice to distinguish between functional and non-functional requirements. The functional requirements are the requirements that talk about what functionality the customer needs. (We'll look at non-functional requirements in the next section.)

There are many different ways to approach requirements gathering:

- Document the business requirements: describe the business processes that the application needs to support.

- Document tasks: describe the tasks that the users of the system need to perform, and what they need to accomplish their tasks.

- Document functionality: describe the exact functionality the application will provide. Which screens there will be, what forms can be filled in and what information will be provided.

A good requirements specification has a healthy mix of these. Using certain functionality, the users will perform certain tasks, that in the end will support a business process. This covers the "why", the "what" and the "how".

There are several ways to document the requirements:

- Use cases. Use cases are a description, usually in the form of a diagram, that describe a certain scenario.

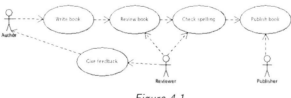

Figure 4.1

- User stories. A user story is similar to a use case, but is written in the form of a short story that describes the scenario. When we cover agile development later on in this book, we'll have a closer look at these.

- Requirements. The 'classic' way of documenting requirements is to define requirements in the form of short sentences, that preferably are numbered so you can reference them in other documents.

Requirements are often created at the beginning of a project, but more often than not, requirements tend to change. Business goals may change, things may happen that change priorities, or you may encounter problems that you hadn't anticipated. All of these things may influence the requirements. Often the customer only knows what he really wants once you've already built it. So it's wise to not set the requirements in stone, but to keep track of them during the project. (Of course, changing the requirements may have influence on the project schedule, your technical design etc., but we'll have a look at that when we cover project management in a later chapter.)

Non-functional Requirements

The non-functional requirements are the requirements that have nothing to do with the functionality, and may directly relate to things that the customer cannot influence. Here are a few examples of non-functional requirements:

- Performance. Your application or web site may need to operate within certain performance parameters, for example in terms of the number of visitors it can handle or the amount of time a user is allowed to wait.

- Scalability. With growth in mind, an application may have to cope with changes in size, amount of users, or amount of data.

- Security. This is always important, but for some applications it's more important than others. A system containing medical records for patients probably has more strict security policies than someone's weblog.

- Reliability. We always try to build applications as reliably as possible, but sometimes we need to pay extra attention to detail. Sites may have a high availability requirement, and this influences the way they are built and hosted. Also, there may be requirements regarding downtime. Web sites targeted at a local audience may be allowed to be down for maintenance at night; for 24x7 applications, downtime should be kept to a minimum and certain maintenance windows may need to be defined.

- Maintainability. You can hack something together, or create a well-designed architecture; this influences the maintainability of an application, and sometimes a customer may have specific requirements in this regard. For example, if they are going to do maintenance, or if they want to remain independent from the company that built the application.

- Compatibility. An application may need to be compatible with an older version. Sometimes, data has to be migrated. It may also have to be compatible to certain industry standards or to some of the existing applications that a customer uses.

As you can see, the non-functional requirements are mostly "...ility" terms (why don't they call it performability?). Customers may not always think of the "...ilities". It's the job of the analyst to make sure that these are covered, because even when the customer doesn't mention them, there are usually "...ilities" that you need to take into account.

Interaction Design

Wireframes

Once you have a clear picture of what you are going to build, it's useful to present it in such a way that the customer can easily understand it. As a picture says more than a thousand words, creating a visual representation of the application before you build it is very helpful.

In the case of a web site or application, these pictures can be created in the form of so-called *wireframes*. A wireframe, as the name implies, is a schematic mockup of a screen. The picture in 4.2 illustrates a wireframe:

In this wireframe, we can see the entire screen as it is going to be, but without layout. It helps clarify the structure of an application and defines how functionality will be placed in the application. It doesn't even matter if the dimensions are right,

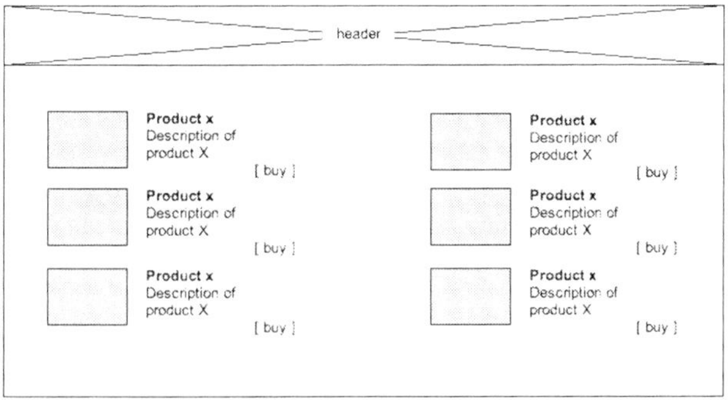

Figure 4.2

a graphic designer will probably change those anyway. As long as the right elements are at the right place, the customer will get a clear picture of how the user of the application or the visitor of the site will interact with the application.

Wireframes can be created with simple tools such as pencil and paper, simple drawing programs, or modeling tools such as Microsoft Visio. There are also programs that are targeted specifically at interaction design. One such program is Axure (http://www.axure.com). In Axure, you can draw wireframes and add the functional requirements and the descriptions of the screens directly to the images. It then allows you to generate a clickable HTML preview of the application that the customer can play with. Additionally, it can also generate a complete functional design document containing all the wireframes and their documentation. It is not a free product, but if you have to create interaction designs a lot, it's worth the investment.

Flowcharts

Another useful tool to help document the structure of a web site is a *flowchart*. A web site flowchart represents the pages in a web site and how they relate to each other. It helps define the "paths" that the user can take through the web site. A simple flowchart may look like that in 4.3:

If a web site is relatively big, it does not make much sense to document each and every page of content. Document the important ones and group pages that belong together. Also, the customer may have a CMS that he can use to add and/or re-arrange pages, so documenting every content page would not be very useful. In-

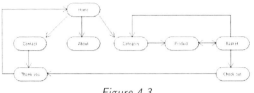

Figure 4.3

stead, document the business critical parts, or the parts that define the important parts of the web site. To give an example, if you have an e-commerce application, just draw one product category page and one product page; it's not useful to create a separate page for every product in the interaction design (also you're not going to code a separate file for each product page anyway).

MoSCoW

A useful addition to the requirements gathering process is performing a so-called *MoSCoW analysis.* The word "MoSCoW" represents the different priorities that requirements may have:

Must-haves

A *must-have* is a requirement that directly supports the business goals. If a must-have isn't implemented, the goals of the project will not be met.

In the case of an e-commerce project, a must-have might be: "the user must be able to add a product to his shopping cart".

Should-haves

A *should-have* is a requirement that, though it is important, does not have to be implemented to meet the business goals. These are typically things for which a workaround is available if they aren't implemented.

An example of this could be 'send to a friend' functionality. While it's very convenient if a site offers the ability to send a page to a friend, and it is interesting functionality in terms of viral marketing, there is a workaround available by manually sending an email containing a link.

Could-haves

Could-haves are requirements that are 'nice', but do not support the business goals. They are intended to make life a little easier, to make the product more fancy. They are requirements that, if time allows it, will be built in, but if time is running out, they will not be implemented. (Or they will be implemented at a later stage, for example in a '2.0' version.)

A could-have example requirement would be to be able to use drag and drop to move an image, instead of ordinary cut and paste. It's nice, but we will not lose any sleep if we don't have it.

Won't-haves

These are the requirements with the lowest priority. It's functionality that we thought of already, but that we know we're not going to build during this project, unless we finish ahead of time and all the must, should and could-haves have been implemented.

Usually, *won't-have* requirements are the type of requirements that come up during a brainstorm session; the features we think are useful to some users, but not really essential to the majority of our users.

(In case you're wondering, the "o"s in MoSCoW don't represent a priority, they just help you remember them.)

Sometimes, customers are going to tell you that everything they require is a must-have. Often this is not the case. If you read the above definitions, there are inevitably requirements that are not really must-have.

An important reason to do a MoSCoW analysis is planning. In an ideal world, where everything goes according to plan, we meet all deadlines and implement all functionality. In reality, things might work out differently. You may run into an unexpected issue and a feature that seemed so simple at first, may take ages to complete. If all your requirements are must-haves, you're in for some trouble. Get out the pizzas and Coke, because you're going to work days and nights to complete all your requirements before the deadline. If on the other hand, you have done a proper MoSCoW analysis, you can trade requirements. You can drop a could-have if a must-have takes more time, so it makes the project more flexible, and you will have less stress throughout the project.

Do realize however, that this takes some understanding between the development team and the customer. I have encountered numerous customers who expected a team to complete all requirements within budget and within the deadline, even the could-haves. It is the project manager's task to manage these expectations. Depending on the situation, you may implement some of the could-haves or even should-haves after the deadline, or move them to a second version of the project.

Chapter 5

Planning

One of the most difficult parts of the software life-cycle is planning. Historically, IT projects have always had the image of always being late and over budget, so planning may not seem very useful. Once the requirements are defined however, a customer usually wants to know what a project is going to cost. Furthermore, we need a plan to be able to assign resources. So even if it's hard, we still have to plan our projects. Let's shed some light on the difficulties of planning.

By the way, if you are a developer and thought you could skip this chapter because planning is something for the project manager, think again. Planning is as much a responsibility of the individual developers as it is of the project manager. The most important part of planning is estimating how much time something is going to take, and this is something that each developer can help determine. To better understand the dynamics of estimates and planning, read this chapter even if you are a developer. It will hopefully make you more aware of your own estimations.

The Planning Paradox

One of the reasons projects are often late and over budget is the *planning paradox*. Suppose you have a PHP application to develop, and it consists of 10 smaller tasks. You create a detailed estimation for each of the tasks and each task is, say, 4 hours. So the complete project can be done in 10 * 4 = 40 hours. Common sense says that if you have to do 10 tasks of 4 hours each, then some of them take a little longer (something may come up), and some of them take less (easier then expected) but on average the task should be possible in 40 hours.

The paradox here is that only the first part is true. Things may go wrong or be more difficult than we expect, and then we need more time. The opposite almost never occurs; if something is easier than expected, we still use 4 hours. So instead of averaging out at 4 hours per task, the average is actually above that, so the total time will be more than 40 hours. Because of this paradox, on average, projects take longer than we initially estimate.

There are a few reasons why this paradox occurs.

- Software is never finished. If you can create something in 4 hours, you can also create it in 6 hours. It will just be nicer.

- It is human nature not to hurry when it's not needed. If you have 4 hours to complete a task, why would you complete it in 3?

There's another way to become aware of this paradox. If someone estimates a task, they are always going to be on the safe side. This means that if they think that realistically they can complete a task in 3 hours, they will build in some margin and estimate it at 4 hours. However, the same effects occur here, and if you execute the task, you are more likely to do it in 4 hours instead of 3.

One way to counter the paradoxical effect is to look differently at the estimations. If the above estimates of 4 hours per task are made in the traditional sense, then chances are that you (maybe subconsciously) think that realistically it can be done in 3 hours, but you added a 1 hour margin 'just to be safe'. By using 4 hours as the basis for the estimation, which got us at 40 hours total, we fall into our own trap and will actually take at least 4 hours per task. Thus we end up not just taking the full 40 hours to complete the project, but probably more.

Now, let's do that differently. If realistically the tasks could be done in 3 hours, let's take 3 hours as our average estimation per task. This gives us a total estimate of 10 * 3 = 30 hours. We add to that a total project margin of 10 hours, so we end up at the same 40. However, we are now less inclined to work 4 hours on each task because our perception of the time available to complete the task has changed. You will notice that you can now complete all the tasks in at least 3 hours.

The paradox still applies, so it's unlikely that something will be less than 3, and probably in half of the cases, we underestimated the task, so those will take a little longer. If half of the tasks take one hour longer, we have a total of 5 additional hours. This is still within our 10 hour margin, so now, by just doing the estimations slightly different, we end up with a total number of hours of 35; 5 below the total 40 we estimated!

A good read on these effects, and ways to cope with it, is the book "Critical Chain" by Eliyahu Goldratt[1]. This book contains a whole project management methodology and is not specific to IT projects, but the parts on planning and estimations are quite useful in PHP projects.

Getting Lost in Details

There is another aspect of estimations that can cause projects to miss deadlines. This has to do with the level of detail we are working with.

Consider the following requirement in a project: "The web site needs to have a contact form so visitors can contact us."

A contact form is a reasonably common sense feature and most PHP developers know how to create one and what should be in it. Depending on several factors, like the overall complexity of the site, the estimations for such a feature may vary. Let's say that a hypothetical developer states that he could build this, completely, with everything that belongs to a contact form, in 4 hours. Sounds reasonable, right?

Now consider the following requirements:

- The web site needs to have a contact form with name, address fields and a text field for the actual message.

- The form should have a 'send' and a 'reset' button.

- If invalid data is entered, the user should get an error message.

- If the data is correct, send the form to the recipient, and show a 'thank you' page.

- If an error occurs, show a 'there was an error, please try again later' page.

- The form should be properly tested.

---

[1] http://www.amazon.com/Critical-Chain-Business-Eliyahu-Goldratt/dp/0884271536

- The form should be integrated in the web site.

If you give this list of requirements to an equally capable developer, he will start to make estimations and tag a number on each of the requirements:

- Basic form handling: 2 hours

- Validation: 1 hour

- Thank you page: 1 hour

- Error page: 1 hour

- Sending form via email: 1 hour

- Testing: 1 hour

- Deploying into existing web site: 1 hour

The total number of hours is now 8 hours, 100% more than in the previous estimation although we're actually creating the same form.

What is happening here is that when planning small tasks, subconsciously developers will calculate with a margin. There's hardly a task smaller than 1 hour because you need time to look into the task, check out the existing sources, think about the solution, etc. Because of this, when each task is estimated individually, they will all contain overhead. Sure if you were to develop just a "submit" button it could take an hour; if you would just develop a thank you page that would take an hour. But if you develop both, it's certainly less than 2 hours.

What in reality is likely to happen here is the following: the first developer, who estimated 4 hours based on the single requirement, has probably not thought of all the details, and may have underestimated it. When not dealing with details, and not encountering the word 'test' or 'delivery' in the requirements, the developer is likely to omit associated tasks from the estimation. In reality, the developer might need 6 hours.

The other developer, who has a total estimate of 8 hours, will probably use at least 8 hours because of the paradox of the previous section.

The solutions to this are:

- Think carefully about the problem. If the requirements are high-level, break them down into details.

- Create a realistic estimate for each of the tasks.

- Add a margin on the complete task (instead of per item).

This solution is remarkably similar to the previous problem. This stems from the fact that the problem has roughly the same cause, which usually has to do with subconsciously calculated overhead, and the fact that it is human nature to work toward a set deadline.

Note that we've been talking about small assignments in this section; however, on the macro scale the same principles apply, so projects of 2,000 hours suffer from the exact same problems as our hypothetical eight hour project.

The Planning Process

Planning is a process. It is something that should be done continuously throughout a project. Often, planning is seen as a one-time activity; we create the plan at the beginning of the project. A project is always dynamic and things change; requirements change, the level of knowledge about the problem domain increases, the relationship with the customer evolves. In short, everything changes; so it's not really useful to stick to an outdated plan. It's better to continuously keep planning the project. Keep an eye on progress, see what has been created so far, and estimate what still needs to be done. Adjust the plan accordingly, and if a deadline is in danger of being missed, take action (like dropping anything less than must-have requirements).

A common mistake in development teams is to take a plan for granted and not update it continuously. Suppose a task was estimated at 10 hours. The developer has been working on the task for 9 hours, and the project manager assumes that we're at 90% completion of the task. However, after 10 hours, the task still isn't finished. It was more difficult than the developer thought, and he needs more time. He looks at the results so far and progress is not so good. In the end, he spends another 10 hours to complete it.

This is where the saying "To complete 90% of the work, takes 90% of the time. To complete the remaining 10%, takes the other 90% of the time" comes from. If planning had been a continuous process in this scenario or, in other words, if we would have continuously looked at the actual progress (and not just the time spent) and at the estimated time to completion, we would have discovered earlier that we were not going to make the deadline, and we could have taken action earlier on in the process, for example by having a senior developer help out.

Not Just Code

A final note in this chapter: there's more to development than just coding. By the time you've finished this book you will realize that writing PHP code is only a part of the entire development life-cycle. Still, estimations often only contain the development parts of a project. Running over budget or missing deadlines can be caused by omitting the estimations for meetings, documentation, design, testing or deployment. Taking these elements into account may make your estimations slightly higher. On the other hand, you should have no problem convincing a customer that the extra time this takes is all spent on improving the quality of the end result, and that any development team that does not estimate this time is very likely to go over budget because of the issues that arise from not taking the time to properly spec an application or test it.

Chapter 6

Architecture

If you build a house, you usually don't just start stacking one brick on top of the other. You could, but by the time you're done, it may well collapse like a house of cards. Normally, an architect will have created blueprints first. Even before the first stone has been placed, he will have made sure that the house, once built, not only fits the requirements, but also lives up to current standards of stability and durability. Software should be no different. Before writing the first line of code, the general architecture of the application should be created.

Design

The technical design of an application is the link between the functional design and the code. Where the functional design answers the 'what' question, the technical design answers the 'how' question. In other words, the functional design is what you show the customer, the technical design is what you show the developers.

In the design all technical questions should be answered. Common elements of a technical design include:

- A database model (Often an Entity-Relationship Diagram; ERD)

- Flowcharts

- Object models

- API descriptions

- Descriptions of connections to external applications

- Technology/tool/component selection

- Implementation guidelines

The *design* maps solutions to the *requirements*. Using the technical design as a guide, the development team should be able to implement all features described in the functional design. Let's look at a few concepts that are useful in the technical design phase.

OO

When designing an application, you are going to have to decide whether you want the application to be developed in an object oriented fashion, or procedurally. In PHP4, object oriented programming was possible, but it was more of a hack. In PHP4, objects were in essence very similar to arrays of data, and the methods were just functions operating on that data. The only useful OO concept available in PHP4 was inheritance.

With PHP5, that changed significantly. PHP now features a true object model with most of the features that a serious object oriented language should have. Also, the performance of OO PHP has increased dramatically from PHP4 to PHP5. In PHP4, if performance was an issue, it was better to code procedurally, as object oriented code had a lot of overhead. In PHP5, this is no longer the case: now the benefits of object oriented code by far outweigh the impact on performance. In some situations, object oriented code is even faster than procedural code.

Let's look at a few basic OO concepts. If you are already familiar with object oriented programming ('OOP'), you can safely skip forward to the paragraph labeled 'UML'. If you have so far coded procedurally, continue to read about some of the basics. If you have so far coded OO in PHP4, you might want to read about some of the concepts below, since some of them are new in PHP5 and can be very useful.

Classes and Objects

The basic building block in an object oriented programming approach is a *class*. A class is a definition of an object. It describes both the data (member variables) of an object, and its behavior (methods). Objects are all around us. A ball is an object that has properties (a diameter, weight, color, position) and methods (you can throw the ball, or you can squeeze it). The methods can influence the properties (if you squeeze the ball, its diameter decreases). There is a distinct difference between a class and an object, and especially for those new to OOP it can be confusing. Think of the class as the definition, where objects are the actual instances of that definition. Take this example:

```
class Ball
{
  private $_color = null;

  public function __construct($color)
  {
    $this->_color = $color;
  }
}

$a = new Ball('red');
$b = new Ball('blue');
```

In this case, `Ball` is the class. It defines the concept of a ball. `$a` and `$b` are objects, they are both instances of a ball.

A thorough explanation of all OO concepts in PHP5 can be found in the official PHP manual (`http://www.php.net/manual/en/language.oop5.php`).

Constructors and Destructors

In the previous example, we have a function called `__construct`. This is called the *constructor* of the class. This method is called whenever we instantiate a new object. In this case, the constructor takes a parameter, which allows us to define the color of a ball when creating balls.

The opposite is a __destructor. It is called whenever an object is destroyed. You can use this to clean up resources, close connections, or anything else you need to do before the object is gone.

Inheritance

The most basic concept in OOP is *inheritance*. Inheritance means that one object 'inherits' functionality from its parent. It 'specializes' the base class. If that doesn't make sense, here's an example. If we were to program object oriented hamburgers, we could have the following class:

```
class Hamburger
{
  public function getIngredients()
  {
    return array('meat', 'bun', 'tomato', 'sauce');
  }
}
```

Now suppose we want to program a cheeseburger. A cheeseburger is a hamburger, but with cheese. So we could have the following class:

```
class Cheeseburger
{
  public function getIngredients()
  {
    return array('meat', 'cheese', 'bun', 'tomato', 'sauce');
  }
}
```

While this would work fine, the problems start when we want to change our burgers. What if we want to add pickles to them? We would have to change both classes. Enter inheritance. With inheritance, we can inherit the functionality of a class and change only those things that are different. Using inheritance, the Cheeseburger becomes:

```
class Cheeseburger extends Hamburger
{
  public function getIngredients()
  {
```

```
    $ingredients = parent::getIngredients();
    $ingredients[] = 'cheese';
    return $ingredients;
  }
}
```

What happens here is that the getIngredients method first calls its parent version, which retrieves all the ingredients that all burgers have in common. Then, we add the extra cheese. When we want to add pickles now, we only have to change the Hamburger class.

Derived classes (which is what we call a class that inherits from another class) can change methods, or add methods. Don't be fooled by the keyword 'extends' in the Cheeseburger class. Although this is the way you define inheritance, you're not limited to extending functionality. You can also change functionality (VeggieBurger may replace 'meat' with 'tofu') or remove functionality (PlainBurger might remove 'sauce').

Access Specifiers

Note the keyword 'public' in the previous example. This is called an *access specifier*. It defines who is allowed to call a method, or in the case of a member variable, who is allowed to access it.

In PHP, there are 3 different access specifiers :

- private: a private method can only be called by the class itself, a private property is only accessible to its own class.

- public: a public method or property is accessible to everyone. Other classes or procedural code can call the public methods of a class.

- protected: this is very similar to private, but it also grants access to derived classes. As a rule of thumb, if you think at some point in time your class is going to be extended by other classes, use the 'protected' keyword on the methods and properties that the extended classes may have to override, because they can't if these are private.

Encapsulation

Private and protected methods are useful for controlling access to properties. Consider the following class:

```
class Account
{
  public $balance;
}

$a = new Account;
$a->balance = -1000;
```

Any piece of code can change the balance of an account, even if there's no record of any transaction. This is dangerous. Using *encapsulation*, we can make sure that the balance is only changed if allowed:

```
class Account
{
  private $balance;

  public function withdraw($amount)
  {
    if ($this->balance - $amount > 0)
    {
      $this->balance -= $amount;
      return true;
    }
    return false;
  }
}
```

In this case, balance can never become negative. We have encapsulated the $balance property to protect it. This is an important concept, as we are still in the design phase, and using techniques like this, we can already built in some form of reliability in the design of the application, before we write code. We just design all objects to have proper encapsulated properties.

A common way to encapsulate member variables is using *'getters'* and *'setters'*. These are small methods that retrieve the value of a property, or change it. If we read from or operate directly on the property, we cannot enforce any business logic.

If we implement getters and setters, even if they are just wrappers initially, we can always later on add business logic, validations and access control.

Interfaces

An interface is a 'contract' that defines what methods a class implements, without actually implementing those methods. If a class implements a certain interface, you can be sure that the methods the interface prescribed will be present. It's like interfaces on a computer. If you know something has a USB interface, you can make assumptions on what you can plug into it.

```
interface IDrawable
{
  public function draw();
}

class Image implements IDrawable
{
  public function draw()
  {
    // draw the image.
  }
}

class Canvas
{
  public function add(IDrawable $element)
  {
    // add something to the canvas
  }
}
```

What we see here is an interface IDrawable. This defines "something that can be drawn". It does not implement functionality, it just defines that anything that is drawable should implement a public draw() method.

The class Image implements this interface. Anybody using this class can rely on the fact that an object of that class will have a draw() method that can be called.

In the Canvas class finally, we use *type hinting* to enforce that the $element parameter of the add method accepts only objects that implement the IDrawable interface. This way, we can make sure that anything added to the canvas can be drawn.

More   information   about   interfaces   can   be   found   at
`http://www.php.net/manual/en/language.oop5.interfaces.php`.

Abstract Classes

An abstract class is very similar to an interface, but instead of just defining the methods, it contains some implementation. It is a class that has already some basic methods implemented, but some of the methods are 'abstract', which means that a derived class should implement them. Abstract classes, as the name implies, cannot be instantiated directly. Only derived classes that provide an implementation for all abstract methods, can be instantiated.

Another important difference between abstract classes and interfaces is that you can extend only one abstract class (PHP does not support multiple inheritance), but you can implement multiple interfaces. Examples can be found at `http://www.php.net/manual/en/language.oop5.abstract.php`.

Static Members

Remember the subtle difference between a 'class' and an 'object' I talked about earlier? A class is the definition, and an object is an instance of a class.

```php
class Hamburger
{
  private static $_count = 0;

  public function __construct()
  {
    self::$_count++;
  }

  public static function getCount()
  {
    return self::$_count;
  }
}

$a = new Hamburger();
$b = new Hamburger();
echo Hamburger::getCount();  // 2
```

This code snippet gives an example of what 'static' does. In this example we count the number of instantiated hamburgers. This is not an object property; not every hamburger has a separate counter. Nor would it make sense to do `$a->getCount()` as $a is just one hamburger.

The counter is static, meaning one counter is tracking all instances of the class `Hamburger`. This way, we can get a counter of all the hamburgers that are instantiated. More examples can be found in the PHP manual at `http://www.php.net/manual/en/language.oop5.static.php`.

Polymorphism

Now we covered the basics, it's time to look at a few advanced concepts that can help you when designing applications in true OO style.

The concept of *polymorphism* is a powerful concept that is best explained with an example:

```php
abstract class Shape
{
  abstract protected function draw();
}

class Triangle extends Shape
{
  protected function draw()
  {
    // draw a triangle
  }
}

class Circle extends Shape
{
  protected function draw()
  {
    // draw a circle
  }
}

$shapes = array();
$shapes[] = new Circle();
$shapes[] = new Triangle();
$shapes[] = new Circle();
```

```
$shapes[] = new Square();

foreach ($shapes as $shape)
{
  $shape->draw();
}
```

Shapes are abstract. We know that a shape can be drawn, but 'shape' itself is an abstract concept that has no real meaning. `Circle`, `Triangle`, `Square` etc. are implementations of shapes that can actually be drawn.

The polymorphism is in the last 3 lines. Here we loop through an array of shapes and without having to know what type of shape we are dealing with, we are just calling its `draw()` method. So even if we add four more types of shape, we only have to implement the classes and give them a draw method. The entire application, which just draws shapes, does not have to be changed in any way since it will just call the `draw` method, regardless of how classes implement it.

This is called *polymorphism* and is a very powerful concept. It avoids evil constructs such as:

```
foreach($shapes as $shape)
{
  if ($shape instanceof Circle)
  {
    drawCircle();
  }
  else if ($shape instanceof Triangle)
  {
    drawTriangle();
  }
  ....
}
```

Magic Methods

The *magic methods* are PHP features that allow for some powerful object oriented constructs. It's not really a pure OO concept and it's not very common in other languages either, but it is a powerful feature that was added in PHP5.

Magic methods are methods that are called automatically by the engine when certain things happen. The most familiar examples are `__construct` and `__destruct`, the methods that are called when an object is instantiated or destroyed. But the more powerful ones are:

- `__get`: this is a method that is called automatically when someone tries to access a property that doesn't exist. A useful application of this is to create virtual properties. We'll look at an example of that in a minute.

- `__set`: the counterpart of _get, which is called when someone tries to change a property that doesn't exist.

- `__call`: this method is called when someone tries to invoke a method on an object that doesn't exist.

There are many more magic methods. I won't cover them all here, but you can find them in the manual at `http://www.php.net/oop5.magic`.

Later on, when we cover Design Patterns, I'll talk about the magic methods a bit more. For now, here's a small example that demonstrates how magic methods can be useful:

```
class Dataholder
{
  private $_data = array();

  public function __get($key)
  {
    return $this->_data[$key];
  }

  public function __set($key, $value)
  {
    $this->_data[$key] = $value;
  }
}

$x = new Dataholder();
$x->someValue = 3;

echo $x->someValue;
```

Take a look at what happens in the last 3 lines. First we instantiate a new `Dataholder` object. Then, we assign the number 3 to a property called `someValue`. However, this doesn't exist as a member, so `__set` will be called, and we can manually handle the assignment. In this case, we store it in an array. But it could also be a database, or it could do some validations first, you name it. In the last line, we echo the value of the property, which still doesn't exist, so `__get` is called and we manually retrieve the value of the property.

Object Lifetime

One very important thing to take into account when designing an application in OO style in PHP, is the lifetime of objects. Whenever someone executes a script, your code is executed, objects are created, and at the end of the script, all objects are destroyed. This is very important. The lifetime of an object is exactly one request. This means that you have to be careful with instantiating many objects; you will have to do so on every request.

Developers with a Java background, especially, tend to over-engineer OO applications in PHP, since they are used to a stateful application where objects live as long as the application is running. When working with a web-based scripting language such as PHP, which has a "stateless nature" (nothing is remembered between requests[1]), objects have a much shorter lifespan. This means that when building complex object hierarchies, you are building an entire tree of objects when a script starts, and the tree will be torn down when the script ends.

UML

The *Unified Modeling Language* is a modeling technique that was created in 1996, and was the result of a unification of several other modeling languages[2]. A modeling language provides developers with a means to visualize the design of an application. One UML diagram can be more clear than three pages of specification. UML is particularly useful for applications that are designed with object orientation. If you would rather program procedurally, there are other methods that are more suitable.

---

[1] Sessions are a way to remember things between requests, but in nature, the web is stateless.

[2] The Wikipedia entry for UML, at `http://tinyurl.com/anyno` contains a detailed history.

Given the fact that object oriented development is more and more common in PHP however, I'm going to assume that for your next application you are going to use object oriented programming.

For a thorough explanation on UML I'll have to recommend that you read up on UML online or using books. I'll give some examples though of some of the more important UML diagrams.

Class Diagram

A *class diagram* depicts the classes of an application and the relationships they have.

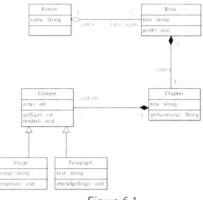

Figure 6.1

In this example diagram, we see several concepts. We can see how a person can write zero or more books. The 'accessor' for the books that a person wrote is called 'bibliography', so eventually in the application we may be able to say:

```
$person->getBibliography();
```

This will give us the list of books a person wrote. In this diagram, we also see inheritance: both Image and Paragraph are derived classes that each derive from Content and add their specific logic. Between Person and Book, there is a 'weak' aggregation; the open diamond indicates that even when an author instance ceases to exist, the book will live on. The relationship between Book and Chapter is 'strong'. The closed diamond indicates a composition: if a Book instance is destroyed, its chapters are destroyed along with it. In the class diagram, for each class the relevant member variables and methods are documented.

Sequence Diagram

In a *sequence diagram*, we can model the method calls that happen between objects. Starting with one call on an object, we see how this triggers calls in related objects, how results are passed back and forth between the objects and how eventually the call results in a certain return value.

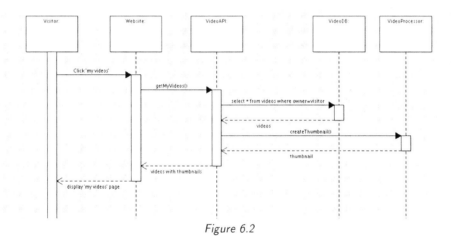

Figure 6.2

In this example of a hypothetical web site for watching videos, we can see the sequence of events that are necessary to show a visitor his "my videos" page. The visitor clicks a link on the web site, which calls a method on an underlying API. The API fetches videos from a database, uses a processor to generate thumbnails, and then passes the result back to the web site, which places the result in a webpage for the visitor. In web applications, I have found sequence diagrams to be particularly useful to document the behavior of APIs.

UML Tools

There are many tools you can use to draw UML diagrams. Some are very basic, others feature things like code generation directly from the UML diagram. Unfortunately, I haven't seen many tools do that for PHP; but now that the new Zend Studio IDE is based on the powerful Eclipse platform, which features the "eclipse modeling framework" (EMF), that is probably a matter of time. Here are a few tools that are useful for generating UML diagrams:

- A whiteboard with some non-permanent markers. When I just start thinking about a project, the ideas in my head aren't stable enough to directly put them down in a modeling tool. I find a whiteboard with markers very convenient in the first phases of the architecture.

- ArgoUML (`http://argouml.tigris.org`). This is a free, open source modeling tool. One of the advantages is that it's cross-platform. I used ArgoUML for some of the diagrams in this book. You need the commercial counterpart 'Poseidon' if you need support for the UML 2.0 specification, but for basic diagrams ArgoUML is sufficient.

- Microsoft Visio (`http://office.microsoft.com/en-us/visio/default.aspx`). Visio has always been a powerful diagram editor.

- Eclipse (`http://www.eclipse.org/`). Keep this one in mind; I foresee powerful integration with Zend Studio.

- Rational Rose (`http://www.ibm.com/software/rational/`). Rational have long been the pioneers in diagramming, and have been bought by IBM a few years ago. The software still bears the name 'Rational Rose'.

Design Patterns

After you have been designing applications for a while, you will start to see patterns. Similar problems in a different context, with similar solutions. Some problems have such common solutions, that they have been given a name. We call these common solutions *design patterns*.

A design pattern is a 'blueprint' for a solution. It's not ready-made code, but a description of a problem and a solution. Most design patterns can be implemented in any language.

If you feel the above concept is too abstract, think of it as a recipe. If your problem is a craving for half-baked fudgy ultra-sweet chocolate (with pieces of nuts), then the solution is the recipe for brownies. While there sometimes are off-the-shelf brownies, the true solution is the recipe, as it will allow you to solve the problem generically and tailored to your specific needs. In software engineering, there are a large number of patterns that have been defined over the years.

There are two books about design patterns that I have to mention. The first is:

- "Design Patterns: Elements of Reusable Object Oriented Software" by the 'Gang of Four' (`http://www.mypearsonstore.com/bookstore/product.asp?isbn=0201633612`) —This book is considered the "Bible" of design patterns. Design patterns first gained popularity when this book appeared. It was one of the most important books during my software engineering study. It contains descriptions of all classic design patterns, with good theoretical background.

- "php|architect's Guide to PHP Design Patterns" by Jason E. Sweat (`http://phparch.com/c/books/id/0973589825`) This book is useful because it not only does a great job of explaining the patterns it covers, it also shows how they are implemented in PHP. Some patterns aren't very practical in PHP (or web applications in general), for example because of the "share nothing" architecture of PHP (every request is handled separately, without persistency of objects). This book covers the ones that are.

Common PHP Patterns

Here are a few common PHP patterns. I won't dive into their implementations or details; they are well documented online, so if you want to explore them further, Google is your friend. (Or check the books I mentioned above.)

- Singleton. Implement this pattern if you want to have only one instance of a certain class. For example the configuration of an application. Note that in

PHP, singletons are slightly different from singletons in many other languages. In PHP, a singleton ensures only one instance per request, it doesn't guarantee that when there are multiple simultaneous requests, there's only one instance of an object. Then again, this is probably the way you would usually want it to work in PHP.

- Factory. A factory creates things. An example of the factory pattern is the situation where you need to instantiate a database connection that depends on a set of variables. Instead of manually creating the instance using the 'new' keyword, you could tell the class to generate an instance for you. A factory is often used to automatically construct the right type of object, or instantiate the right subclass, based on the situation.

- MVC. The 'Model, View, Controller' pattern deals with separation of business logic, presentation logic and application logic. It's an important pattern in PHP so I'll cover it in more detail later on in this chapter.

- Iterator. Iterator is a generic way of looping through things. Usually you loop through arrays, but with the iterator pattern you can loop through anything that can be iterated (database results, collections, vectors, etc.)

- Observer. If you want to trigger things in one object, when something happens in another object, you can implement the observer pattern, which makes one class listen to changes in the other and then act upon it. An example is sending an email when the order status changes. The key feature of the observer pattern here is that you don't have to clutter the `Order` class with this functionality, but can have a separate `ConfirmationMail` class that observes changes in `Order` and acts upon it.

One last word about singletons, everybody who has done database connections in PHP has been tempted to make his database connection class a singleton that you reuse throughout the script. When you first encounter the need to connect with multiple databases (larger applications with multiple data sources, migrations from one database to the other, etc.) you will run into a problem when your connection is a singleton. Usually, for databases it's better to use a *registry of connections* (which is also a pattern).

Magic Methods and Design Patterns

I promised to get back to magic methods in this chapter. A few pages back we looked at the __get, __set and __call magic methods. (If you skipped that part, now is a good time to go back and read it). These methods make it possible to implement several patterns generically.

One pattern I would like to demonstrate is the *decorator* pattern. What the decorator pattern solves can be guessed from its name. It 'decorates' an object. Suppose you have an object that outputs text:

```
class HelloWorld
{
  public function text()
  {
    return 'Hello World';
  }

  public function doSomething()
  {
    doSomeStuff();
  }
}
```

Now suppose we have a situation where we want the output of some of the methods to be in bold. We could implement that in the HelloWorld class, but that would unnecessarily clutter it (OK, for just one method that would be arguable, but imagine we also want italic output, bold italic output, reverse output, etc.)

The clean solution to this is the decorator pattern. It would roughly be implemented like this:

```
class BoldDecorator
{
  private $_object;

  public function __construct($object)
  {
    $this->_object = $object;
  }

  public function text()
```

```
    {
      return '<b>'.$this->_object->text().'</b>';
    }

    public function doSomething()
    {
      return $this->_object->doSomething();
    }
  }
```

We can pass an object to its constructor, and this object will then be decorated. So this code will output "Hello World" in bold:

```
$a = new HelloWorld();
$b = new BoldDecorator($a);
echo $b->text();
```

$b behaves exactly the same as $a, but when we call text(), the output is bold. The only disadvantage is that to make $b behave like $a, we also had to implement the doSomething method, even though we aren't doing any customizations to that.

Now suppose HelloWorld had many more methods than just 'text' and 'doSomething'. To be able to truly decorate the object, we would have to implement all its methods, and the BoldDecorator will become very tightly coupled to the HelloWorld class. Every time we add a new method to HelloWorld, we have to add it to BoldDecorator too.

This is where the magic methods are useful. Here's the same BoldDecorator, but this time using the __call magic method:

```
class BoldDecorator
{
  private $_object;

  public function __construct($object)
  {
    $this->_object = $object;
  }

  public function text()
  {
    return '<b>'.$this->_object->text().'</b>';
```

```
  }

  function __call($method, $args)
  {
    return call_user_func_array(array($this->_object,
                                      $method), $args);
  }
 }
```

This way, the BoldDecorator is more generic. We only implement the method we're decorating ('text'), and any other method call is automatically forwarded to the underlying object using the __call magic method. The decorator pattern is just one example of a generic solution that can easily be implemented using PHP's magic methods, but there are many more.

You might wonder why we don't just extend HelloWorld with a BoldHelloWorld subclass; the main benefit from using the Decorator pattern here is that we can chain multiple decorators (consider an italic bold helloworld, that's not possible with inheritance). Another benefit is that the generic Decorators are reusable for other classes.

Please note that the above code isn't really complete yet, there are several other things we need to take care of, such as access to properties. On my blog, I have an article that covers design patterns with magic methods in more detail: http://www.jansch.nl/2006/07/03/building-proxies-decorators-and-delegates-in-php5

The above examples demonstrate the so-called "genericness" of design pattern solutions. If you are creating the design of an application, take design patterns into account, so you're not reinventing the solution for common problems.

Enterprise Patterns

Aside from the basic patterns mentioned above, there's a set of design patterns that are a little more advanced, and that are especially useful in bigger, more complex, applications. Here are a few :

- ActiveRecord. This pattern maps a database to an object, in such a way, that the underlying SQL is abstracted away from the application code. The developer manipulates an object, sets some of its properties, and the object itself will handle its persistence, in other words, it will store itself in the database or read its own data when needed.

- Proxy. A proxy can be used to prevent direct access to an object, for example to improve performance by instantiating the object only when needed. The proxy can be a lightweight placeholder that mimics the underlying object, but that defers instantiating that underlying object until it actually has to. Another application of proxies is wrapping functionality around an object, for example a security layer or a caching layer.

At the PHP Quebec conference 2008, Stefan Priebsch gave a lecture on Enterprise PHP Patterns. It gives an overview of some of the more advanced patterns that are useful in PHP. Preferably, you should see the presentation in real life, but his slides can be found at: `http://static.e-novative.de/presentation/EnterprisePHPPatterns.pdf`.

Database Design

The software itself isn't the only important part of an application that requires a proper design. The database is just as important, if not more important. Eric Raymond used to say[3]: "Smart data structures and dumb code works a lot better than the other way around", which means that if the data model is well thought out, the code will be a lot cleaner and easier to maintain.

ERD

The common way to design a database is to create an *Entity Relationship Diagram* or ERD. The ERD defines all the tables and their relationships. The level of detail you need in an ERD depends on the application and the complexity. I usually put the tables, the relationships between them, and the important fields (the primary keys and several other significant fields) in the diagram. If the functional design already is clear about the necessary data fields, I don't bother copy/pasting them to the ERD. However, if the functional design did not yet decide what fields are needed, and the

---

[3]The quote is from The Cathedral and The Bazaar, `http://tinyurl.com/48lcbk`

ERD is going to be used by the developers to implement the database, then it's better to have the highest level of detail, and also document the fields and their types.

Figure 6.3 is an example of an ERD diagram:

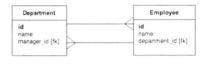

Figure 6.3

In this example, we see two tables ("entities"), "Department" and "Employee". There are two one-to-many relationships in this diagram: one department can contain multiple employees. If an employee is a manager, he can manage multiple departments.

There are several different notations you can use to create an ERD. I'm used to the *crowfoot* notation for indicating one-to-many relationships, but there are other accepted methods. Pick one that feels right and stick to it.

Often, an ERD is skipped and the data model is implemented directly in the database. While this may be acceptable for small applications of only a few tables, for most applications it's better to have an ERD. Here are a few reasons:

- For new developers, an ERD gives a clear overview of the data model that can easily be understood. Wading through the code and looking at the database takes a lot more time to get to know a data model.

- Having the database drawn in a data model gives a better picture of the correctness of the data model, as relationships are visualized instead of hidden in code.

- It is very useful if you need to make changes afterward. Seeing the current model and changing it in the model is far easier than changing it directly in the database. In the model you can more easily see where new parts should go, if there aren't already existing parts that are affected etc.

It helps when you need to get some data from the database. The ERD can tell you visually what query you are going to have to do and which joins to perform. Without an ERD, it's more guesswork or it takes more looking at the database structure.

Note that, like the rest of the design, it's important to keep it up to date. An out-dated design is almost as bad as no design at all. The best way to make changes to the data model of an application is to first change the ERD, and then change the database accordingly. This has the lowest chance of mistakes.

Relationships

Designing a database is all about relationships. If you have a database that supports it, create relationships at the database level by creating foreign key constraints. Many PHP development teams have started out with MySQL years ago and are used to not specifying any relational integrity constraints at the database level, simply because MySQL didn't feature this. Nowadays it does, and it's a good thing to take into ac-count when designing the database. If you specify foreign key constraints, you can ensure relational integrity at the database level, so no application or manual query can break this. Developers used to database servers such as Oracle or DB2 are prob-ably already familiar with foreign key constraints. If so, feel free to skip to the next section.

If you're not familiar with the term *relational integrity*, it's the concept of knowing that the relationships in your database are correct. If you have one table called order with a field called customer_id which references the customer table, then relational integrity makes sure that if there's a customer_id in an order record, it points to an ac-tual customer. This means that if you delete a customer that has orders, the database will take action to keep the referential integrity intact. What action it takes depends on the type of foreign key:

- On Delete Cascade. When a relationship has this type of foreign key con-straint and a record is deleted, the database will delete any records that ref-erence the deleted record. For example, if you delete a customer with a certain customer_id, all orders of that customer will be deleted along with it. This is usually used in so-called "strong associations," meaning situations where you can say that one entity 'owns' the records in the other entity (also often called master-detail relationships).

- Restricted Delete. This is the opposite. A restricted delete will prevent the deletion of a record if there are any records that reference the record. In the customer/order example, with a restricted delete constraint, deleting the customer would fail if there are still orders for this customer.

- On Delete Set Null. In this case, if a record is deleted that was referenced by other records, the referencing records are updated so they no longer reference the record. Their foreign key values are set to null. If you have a manager-employee relationship, and the manager quit, the manager record gets deleted. This doesn't mean that his employees will be deleted too (cascade); it also doesn't mean someone will tell the manager that he can't quit because of his team (restricted). It means that the employees will be updated and will no longer have a manager.

The syntax of how to apply foreign key constraints varies from database to database, and we're also still in the design phase, so I won't cover that here. You'll have to consult your DBA or your database documentation to see how you can implement foreign key constraints. In the design phase, it's important to think about these relationships, as it defines the behavior of your application when data is deleted.

Constraints

The foreign key constraints guard the relationship between data. But the data itself also needs to be guarded sometimes. For example, a birth date needs to be valid, a number field must be within a certain range, a text field may only contain a specific value. You can implement validations at the application level, but you can also define constraints in the database. That is, if the database supports it. MySQL 5 currently doesn't: it accepts the syntax of constraints but won't enforce them). Oracle and DB2 do. If you use a different database, you will have to check the documentation.

A so-called *constraint* may look like this:

```
ALTER TABLE order ADD CONSTRAINT discount_rng CHECK (discount < 100);
```

In this case, the discount field in the order table may not exceed 100 so nobody can add a discount that is more than the price of the order. Most databases allow you to give the constraint a name, which is discount_rng in this case.

The advantage of constraints at the database level is that it ensures that all data is valid. If constraints are enforced at the application level, then there is a higher risk that they will break if the application is changed, if someone creates new functionality that doesn't implement the validation, and if some other application is used to manipulate data, the data might become invalid. Constraints at the database level prevent that.

Triggers and Stored Procedures

Triggers and stored procedures are another feature that can help with data integrity. Where constraints merely check the value of fields, triggers can be used to actively update data when things happen in the database. A trigger fires before, after or instead of an event, and an event can be the insert, delete or update of a record. An example of a trigger is updating the total order amount in the order table whenever a new item is added to an order. Most databases support triggers; MySQL supports them since version 5.0.2.

Stored procedures, simply put, are to a database what functions are to PHP. Procedures contain database logic that can be called from a trigger or constraint, from a query or directly in an SQL prompt. Like triggers, stored procedures are a way to place business logic in the database. Storing business logic in the database might seem like a bad idea, but sometimes it isn't. If you have a database that will be used by a variety of applications or a mix of technologies (PHP, Java, reporting tools) and want to ensure that certain business logic is enforced at all times, placing the business logic in the database is a good solution. In the design phase, it's useful to think carefully about how and when to use triggers and stored procedures. Documenting them in the technical design document is important, as it will guide the development team in the correct application of business logic.

Normalization

A database is in general considered normalized if the data model is free of duplications or redundancies. There are several levels (several so-called "normal forms"), each adding a more strict set of rules to the way the data model is designed. There are entire books on the subject of database design, so I won't go into it too deeply here.

One thing I do find important to mention is *denormalization*. Often, to increase performance, data models are denormalized; redundancy is introduced to prevent joins. In general, this is a bad idea. If you run into performance issues with a database, first look at optimizing the queries, applying indexes or other ways to increase performance. Only as a last resort should you consider de-normalizing the data model. If you do, take the following things into account:

- Document the parts that you de-normalize, as they are more prone to errors when maintenance is done or modifications are made.

- Ensure integrity at the lowest level. If you need to duplicate some data into a separate flat table for performance reasons, keep that table up to date using triggers, so you rule out discrepancies in the data.

Near the end of the book, I've dedicated an entire chapter to optimization, so let's leave it at this for now.

ORM

If your applications are developed using object orientation, but your database is relational, you will have to find a way to combine those two concepts. Mapping an object model to a relational database is called an *Object-Relational Mapping* (ORM).

The simple case is a single class that has a few properties. This is implemented in the database as a single table that has columns for the properties that need to be stored. Design patterns like ActiveRecord help solve this problem and there are also some libraries and tools in PHP that do some of the work needed when mapping objects to records. (Propel is an example and we'll look at it in the Building Blocks chapter later in this book).

Often object models are more complex than just single classes that can be mapped to database tables. It's easy to create a table that holds the data for such a simple class, but what about inheritance, how do we handle that at the database level? This can be challenging, and there are multiple ways to map the object model to the database. Consider the UML diagram in Figure 6.4.

The application from this model deals with persons, represented by the `Person` class, which contains all the logic that every `Person` has in common. Then, we have

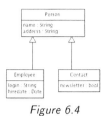

Figure 6.4

two derived classes which extend `Person`: `Employee` and `Contact`. An employee has a user account for the application, and some fiscal information we need to keep track of. A contact person on the other hand has some commercial data attached to them.

There are three ways to map this model to a database. Which solution is best depends on the situation (and sometimes on the library or tools you use; for example Propel only supports the first of the methods we will look at). Let's look at the options and their advantages and disadvantages. Weigh your requirements against these advantages and disadvantages, and select the option that works best in your situation. Note that it's possible to mix several solutions in one application, depending on the situation, but be aware that this will raise complexity and will make it more difficult for the development team to properly implement.

Base-table

Tables needed: 1

Figure 6.5

The entire model is modeled into a single table. The `type` field is the "discriminator": it can be used to store whether a record is an "employee" or a "contact".

Depending on the type, either the `login` and `hiredate` fields are filled (employee case) or the `newsletter` field is filled (contact case).

Advantages:

- Easy to understand.

- Easy to manipulate.

- Fast (no joins required to retrieve data from the base class and the derived class simultaneously)

- It's easy to do queries on base-class level, e.g. retrieve the name of all persons, regardless of whether they are an employee or a contact.

- An object can change type by just changing the discriminator field and fill in the proper data fields.

Disadvantages:

- If the number of derived classes is large, there will be a large number of columns, many of which will not be used most of the times. 'select *' queries will be inefficient because of this.

- You cannot put 'not null' constraints on any of the subclasses' fields: if you would make hiredate `not null`, even though it is a required field for employees, you could no longer store contacts in the table. This can be solved with constraints such as `type<>'employee' OR hiredate IS NOT NULL` but that is significantly less convenient.

- The table structure can be confusing with a more complex data model

- If you have many employees and many contacts, you will end up having very large tables, as they contain records of different meaning.

If you apply this method for mapping inheritance to a data model, consider adding a number of views; if you create one view per derived class (a view called 'Employee') that contains only the fields that belong to the derived class, you negate some of the above disadvantages.

Specialized tables

Tables needed: One per derived class (two in our example)

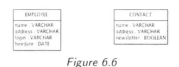

Figure 6.6

In this case, the fields from the base-class are placed in both tables. If there are only a few fields that the derived classes have in common, and you seldom need to retrieve data from both tables simultaneously, this is a good option.

Advantages:

- While `Person` and `Employee` are 2 classes, in the database they are stored in a single table, which makes retrieving employee data, including its base class information, very straightforward.

- There is no "wasted space" in columns that aren't used.

- Data is distributed over 2 tables, which can have performance benefits.

Disadvantages:

- A change in the base-class (e.g. an extra field) will require you to change all the derived tables.

- If you need to query on the base class level (e.g. retrieve all names for all persons), you will need to use unions. This will make the queries more complex, and reduce performance.

- This approach does not offer the opportunity to change the model in such a way that a person can be both an employee and a contact. It would require a record in both tables, duplicating the base fields.

- Similarly, switching the type on a record will require you to move data from one table to the other.

Here too, database views are useful; the disadvantage of having to use a union can be slightly negated by creating a "Person" view that does this for you (this is more convenient, but not faster).

Normalized model

Tables needed: One per derived class, plus one for the base class (three in our example)

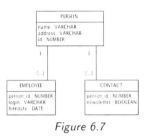

Figure 6.7

In this model the shared data is placed in a base table, and the fields that are specific to a certain type are placed in separate tables. The base table may or may not have a discriminator field, depending on your needs.

Advantages:

- This is the most normalized version of the three models.

- The design is clear; and it's easy to understand what data goes where.

- This model allows easy and fast access to just the base table, if you need it (no unions required).

- You can use lazy loading; load the records from the base table only first, and as soon as you need additional specific data depending on the type of record, you can load this data on the fly. (For this to work, you will need to add a discriminator field to the base table)

- The specific data is distributed over several tables, which can be more efficient.

Disadvantages:

- If you frequently need all fields of an employee, including the base fields, you are going to have to join the tables a lot. Joins are relatively expensive from a performance point of view.

- It is hard to enforce the rule that a person cannot have data in both tables; this would require a check in one table upon insert of a record into the other.

- As with the other solutions, there's a benefit you can get from views here: in this case you can create a view that does the join between base and specific table for you for easier access of the full employee or contact data. While this is more convenient, note that it still needs to perform the join so although views can optimize this a bit, it's still an important disadvantage.

High Level Architecture

So far in this chapter, we've covered some of the basics you need to take into account when designing an application. There is a "higher level," a more abstract way to think about applications, and choosing a "high level architecture" will have a significant impact on the application and its surroundings. It defines an overall concept. For example, if you say "our application follows an SOA architecture," it not only sounds cool, but it actually defines how the foundations of the application are built.

MVC

The most common architecture in PHP applications right now is the *MVC* architecture, which stands for "Model, View, Controller." MVC is actually a design pattern, a common solution for a common problem.

When PHP was gaining popularity years ago, most people were mixing PHP code with HTML output. It didn't take long for people to realize that this wasn't such a good idea, as changes in layout were very difficult to accomplish without harming the PHP code. Pretty soon, people started using template engines to separate the layout from the code. The template contained the layout, and the code was written around that.

As applications became bigger, this 2-layer approach was reaching its limits, and over time, people started using the MVC paradigm.

Here's a short explanation of the three components of an MVC architecture:

- Model. This is the part of the application that contains the "business logic."

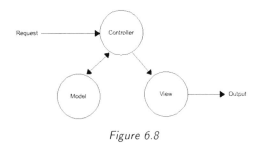

Figure 6.8

- View. This represents the user interface, commonly the templates. In other words: "presentation logic."

- Controller. This is what actually makes an application out of the Model and the View; it contains "application logic."

Models are usually reusable by multiple controllers and views. If you have trouble determining what should be considered a View, a Controller or a Model, just remember one example that you can easily remember. I always use the example of a hotel reservation system. The most important Model in a hotel reservation system is a Reservation. It contains information on what has been booked, who the customer is, what the price is. This contains all the business logic. If you want to know what a reservation costs, the Reservation model is the component to talk to.

The Views are the pages that display the reservation data to the user, that put the data from the model in a template. In the view the decision is made whether or not to display the price in bold, where to put the picture of the hotel room etc.

The Controller in a hotel reservation system is the software that ties the Model and the Views together, and that makes sure that the user can make a reservation by navigating from one step through the next. As the customer progresses through the booking, the Model is updated (the dates are set, the prices are calculated, the room is reserved) and Views are displayed (every step in the reservation process).

Although MVC stands for 'Model, View, Controller', there's usually more than one of each. In the hotel example, you could have a separate model for working with the hotel room (updating and checking its availability), one for working with a reservation and one for working with customers (adding customers, validating addresses).

If you have a lot of application logic, you can even have multiple controllers handling different parts of the application (a reservation controller, a search controller etc.)

I want to pay some extra attention to the model, as it is an important part of larger PHP applications. Often, the model is confused with the database. There are many frameworks that claim to be an 'MVC framework', but have a model which is nothing more than a database abstraction layer. For some applications, there isn't much business logic other than the data in the database. In this case a 'thin model', a small wrapper around the database, will suffice. But often, there is more business logic, and developers are tempted to put this logic in the controller. This is not the correct place. In that case, move towards a 'thick model' that contains not only access to the data, but also enforces the business rules. In the hotel reservation example, calculating the price and checking if a room is available, are examples of business logic that should go in the model, not in the controller. This will help you keep things structured, and will also promote reuse of the model in different parts of the application, or even between applications.

A final note: databases do not have to be the only source of data; you can just as easy create a model around a web service.

Multi-tier Development

The MVC approach has a logical separation of business, presentation and application logic, but they are usually physically located on the same machine, and are consolidated in a single code-base.

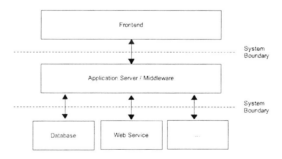

Figure 6.9

When applications grow, there's a point where it starts making sense to have a physical separation as well.

The most common physical separation is between database and web server. As soon as an application becomes too big for a single server, the first way to spread the application over 2 servers is to have the database on a separate machine.

For bigger applications, the logical next step is to distinguish between 3 physical tiers:

- The front-end. This is the application layer responsible for business logic.

- The application server. Where the application logic and business logic resides

- The data layer. Either a database or a web service.

If there is a physical separation between the tiers, you need a way to communicate from one layer to the next. There are several ways to do this.

- SOAP. The 'Simple Object Access Protocol' is designed to be able to call functionality remotely. SOAP can be used between the application server and the data layer, and/or between the front-end and the application server.

- REST. The 'Representational State Transfer' protocol is lighter than SOAP, and very useful between the application server and the front-end. REST is based on ordinary HTTP requests (get, post, put and delete). Using REST, the application layer can churn out XML, JavaScript or HTML snippets, which can easily be used in the front-end. It can also use so-called 'JSON' encoded objects (the 'JavaScript Object Notation') to transport PHP objects from the application server to the front-end, where they live on as JavaScript objects.

- Native protocols; if the data tier is a database, you can use direct database connections to communicate.

A common scenario where multi-tier development is applied, is in enterprise portals. The front-end server is merely a wrapper that displays so-called 'portlets'. The portlets are generated by the application layer and retrieve their data from the data layer. As the complexity of an application increases, you can add more layers, but in most situations you will find three layers.

There are several advantages to having a physical separation in tiers:

- It promotes clean design; you are forced to think about what layer functionality belongs in.

- It eases team development; by defining proper API's between the tiers, people in a development team can more easily divide the work. Instead of all working on the same code-base at the same time, some can work on the front-end, some on the application tier, etc.

- Each tier can be built on hardware that is targeted at the type of software that it runs. The front-end servers can be optimized as a web server, while the application server can be optimized for processing business logic.

It is a very scalable solution. Every tier can separately grow. If there are a lot of visitors, you will have a lightweight front-end distributed over a number of servers, that caches the data it receives from the application server, so you need less servers in that tier. If there's heavy load on the database (e.g. with transaction oriented web sites), you can scale just the database tier.

SOA

The final step in separating an application is a Service Oriented Architecture. In an SOA, applications are comprised of services. Services have a specific set of functionality, and offer that functionality through a well-defined API to other services. In an order management system, you might have a service handling customer addresses, a service handling billing, a service handling payments, etc. So-called brokers connect the services, and the application merely consists of a set of services glued together. More and more off-the-shelf applications offer their services not only via a GUI, but also via a web service. Smart applications can use this to connect to these services to create powerful connections between applications.

Services in an SOA environment usually work via the SOAP protocol. The services that web applications provide via the SOAP protocol are generally called 'web services'.

SOA is associated more often with Java than with PHP, but PHP is a very suitable language for service oriented architectures: PHP5's SoapClient class makes it easy to implement a SOAP client, so building an application that makes use of web services is not complex. It takes only a few lines of code to consume a web service in PHP.

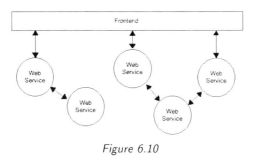

Figure 6.10

Similarly, creating a web service is easy using PHP's `SoapServer` class. Using the `SoapServer`, you can turn any class into a web service.

The general advantages of a Service Oriented Architecture are:

- Even more scalable than multi-tier development; in multi-tier development a tier can be scaled if necessary, in an SOA every service can be scaled individually.

- Increased testability; every service has a well-defined API and can be (automatically) tested.

- Component reuse; services are usually generic so they can be used in other applications and/or combined with other services in a clean way.

- Improved reliability; each service can separately be fixed or changed. Services can be replaced with other services if they no longer fulfill the needs of the application. As long as the APIs are left intact, this is a very smooth process too.

An important aspect to take into account with an SOA is that there is some performance overhead incurred in consuming or providing a web service. This overhead is caused by the SoapClient and SoapServer having to interpret and generate XML messages. There is also some overhead in network usage, as the services need to communicate with each other. In return for this overhead however, an SOA has the ability to run many services in parallel. While one server is looking up the customer's address information, another server can simultaneously retrieve the corresponding billing information.

An SOA can become complex: properly design the architecture from the start, by answering the following questions:

- What services do you need?

- Which component is going to provide what services?

- How is it going to do that?

- What is the required API for each component?

By answering these questions in the technical design, you will get a clear picture of your Service Oriented Architecture before you start building the components.

Guidelines

One goal of defining an architecture for an application is to provide guidelines that can be used during development. The guidelines define the frame of reference for the code. For example, if the application needs to focus on performance, this has to be taken into account in all parts of the code base.

As opposed to coding standards and other guidelines that are usually defined at company level, the architectural guidelines are often project specific. In the technical design you can reference the company guidelines, such as coding standards, that should be followed in throughout the project, and you can specify any specific project guidelines that need to be taken into account. These guidelines include:

- Performance. I will cover optimization in a later chapter, but sometimes you have very specific performance requirements, and you will have to provide guidelines in the technical design on how to meet the performance requirements.

- Usability. It is a good thing to outline some general usability rules that all functionality should adhere to.

- Consistency. If two forms in the same application behave differently, this will confuse users; by providing guidelines on how to handle form validation, user feedback, error reporting etc., you will get a more consistent application over-all.

Chapter 7

Tools

Ever since we descended from the trees, we've been building tools. Tools help us become more productive, and help us achieve things that would've been impossible without tools.

For PHP developers, there's a whole array of tools that are useful. We've already covered some tools when we talked about requirements and architecture, but now is a good time to focus on the tools that will help us during the rest of the development process.

Editors

If you want to program PHP, a basic editor is all you need to be able to write PHP. And there are many to choose from. It sometimes seems there are more editors than there are developers.

I was a fan of SciTE (`http://www.scintilla.org/SciTE.html`) for many years, as it was very easy to use yet powerful. It was as simple as notepad, but offered syntax highlighting for SQL, HTML, XML, JavaScript, CSS and PHP (and others, but those are the ones you need most as a PHP developer), a powerful search with regular expression search and replace, hooks for firing up a browser to test the code. Nowadays, most editors targeted at developers have similar functionality.

Editors such as EditPlus and UltraEdit are fairly well-known, and for the Mac, TextMate (`http://macromates.com/`) is a powerful alternative.

There are also many command line editors, which are useful if you need to edit directly on a (development) server (don't ever edit directly on a production environment; more on that later in this book). There's the legendary Emacs and the ever-present Vi, which both take some time to master, but once you get to know them, they are very powerful. For developers that don't like the torture of learning Emacs or Vi, there are many lighter command line editors: Joe, Pico or Nano.

When selecting a text editor, there are a few features you will want to pay attention to:

- Syntax highlighting; preferably not just for PHP, but for JavaScript and HTML as well.

- Powerful search and replace. Being able to search not only in the current file but in the entire project file structure helps finding your way around a code base. A powerful replace functionality is essential when refactoring large portions of code.

- The ability to open multiple files at once; you'll be working on bigger projects with many files; having to open one file at a time quickly becomes annoying. (I like tabbed editors, but that's mostly a matter of preference.)

- Support for line-endings other than the one your operating system supports. In other words, if you work on a windows machine but edit files on a Linux server, make sure the line-endings are preserved, or your files can come out pretty garbled.

A very extensive comparison of text editors can be found on Wikipedia at `http://en.wikipedia.org/wiki/Comparison_of_text_editors`.

Integrated Development Environments (IDEs)

While text editors are useful at times, and often the only thing available on a server, I would strongly recommend the use of an *Integrated Development Environment* for development. IDEs, as the name implies, integrate an editor with a large set of other tools. Most IDEs support the following features on top of a text-editor:

- Debugging. This gives you the ability to step through an application line by line. This feature is so important and useful that I'll spend some more time on it later in this chapter.

- Code completion. If you type a few letters, it will auto-complete the rest. This will not only help prevent carpal-tunnel syndrome, it will prevent typos and can help prevent code duplication (if you can find the functions easily, you're less likely to reinvent the wheel).

- Syntax highlighting. While only some text editors feature this, all IDEs do. Syntax highlighting displays the code in different colors, which makes it easier to read. It will also reduce naming conflicts as standard PHP functions are usually highlighted in a distinct color.

- Project support. An IDE lets you open an entire project, which includes all the files that belong to the project. This makes it easy to navigate through a code base.

- Inline documentation. Most IDEs have a function key that you can press when the cursor is on a function or class, to open up an integrated or online help. Some IDEs automatically show documentation when typing the name of a function. Most IDEs also give hints for parameters. When entering the parameters to a function, the IDE will tell you what parameter to enter. This way, you don't have to remember or look up the correct order of parameters.

- Cross-referencing. If you call a function from elsewhere in the project, most IDEs let you `ctrl/cmd/alt/etc-click` the function name to directly jump to its definition.

- Source control integration. Most IDEs let you check-in/check-out/update files directly from a source code repository such as SVN or CVS (later on in this chapter we'll have a closer look at source control).

- Profiling. Some IDEs feature a profiler, that can help detect performance or memory issues. A performance profiler tracks function calls and shows bottlenecks in a script, a memory profiler shows what parts of the code are consuming too much memory.

- Templates and code snippets. Many IDEs have a library of common code snippets. Typing a few characters is enough to inject loops, switches, database connections or other common items into your file. If the templates can be customized, you can create specific templates for your company or project. An example of this is the header documentation for your files. Write it once, and store it as a template that you can easily inject into new files.

- Syntax checking. PHP is not a compiled language; this means that we don't get compiler feedback like we do in compiled languages such as Java or C. So typos are often discovered when it's too late. Some IDEs solve this problem by adding syntax checking as functionality. Before you finish the code and before you test it, you can have the IDE check the syntax for typos. It will report any misspelled variables, missing semicolons, unused parameters and even the use of "=" when you really meant to use "==". Some IDEs do this in realtime, while you are typing: this is very similar to spelling checks in word processors.

- WYSIWYG editing. IDEs often feature a graphical editor for HTML templates. I prefer to use the best tool for the job (which usually means I use a dedicated HTML editor), yet there are situations where it's useful to be able to visually edit the templates of an application.

- Database support. An Integrated Development Environment wouldn't be complete if it didn't also integrate database development. Many IDEs therefore support database manipulation.

- Inspection. Many IDEs will let you visually inspect classes, to see what properties and methods they offer.

- Refactoring. "Search and Replace" is one way to refactor code, but some IDEs have a smarter solution. Refactoring can rename classes and variables in a safe way. If you have a function called `hello()` and a variable called `$hello`, a search and replace for "hello" would replace both the function and variable. Refactoring lets you rename just the variable or just the function, and will change all references (even in other files) correctly without touching the code it shouldn't.

Well, that's nearly one and a half page of features that IDEs offer that most editors don't. Still using a text editor? You may want to reconsider that. IDEs are usually targeted at increasing productivity, and can be real time savers. They have a slightly steeper learning curve than editors, but the additional benefits are well worth it.

I often meet developers that are using an IDE, but who are unaware of most of the above features. They tend to use the IDE as a luxurious text editor, and only use a few (or maybe none) of the above features. If that's you, spend some time learning your IDE and making use of the features that it offers. You will reap the benefits within days.

There are several IDEs to choose from. Here are a few examples:

- Zend Studio; `http://www.zend.com/en/products/studio`

- NuSphere PhpED; `http://www.nusphere.com/products/phped.htm`

- Eclipse PDT; `http://www.eclipse.org/pdt/`

- Komodo; `http://www.activestate.com/Products/komodo_ide/index.mhtml`

Selecting an IDE is like selecting a car. A part of the decision is based on the features it offers, but a large part is based on the feeling you get when developing in the IDE, and the comfort it offers.

Most IDEs are commercial products, but the price is peanuts compared to the gain in productivity. Depending on your hourly rate, the return on investment on an IDE is typically a matter of hours, not even days (as in, if you save 5 hours in a year, you've already won back the investment, and if you save more, you start saving money). Many IDEs offer an evaluation version. Before you settle on an IDE, make sure you test it for a while in an actual project.

Debugging

Debugging is literally: "getting the bugs out of the code". There are many ways to do that. The most effective is probably to avoid getting bugs in the application in the first place, but I have yet to encounter a bug-free developer, no matter how senior they are. There are some great tools to do debugging, but let's first have a look at the classic ways to debug.

Alt-tab Debugging

You've written a piece of code, and when you test it in your browser, you notice it doesn't work. So you `alt-tab` back into your editor, make a few changes, `alt-tab` back to the browser, hit reload, and check if it now works. If it doesn't, you `alt-tab` back again and so on and so forth.

I like to call this "alt-tab" debugging, and despite being rather inefficient, it's very common. For Mac users this would be called "command-tab" debugging, and in non-web development this is also often referred to as "shotgun debugging". It's like shooting at a moving target with a bug shotgun. You might hit, but you're more than likely to miss.

Echo Debugging

Another popular form of debugging in PHP is *echo debugging*. When looking for a bug, you insert `echo`, `var_dump` and/or `print_r` statements between the code to see what it's doing. While this may work in a development environment, you really don't want to do this when finding a problem on a live environment. Both "alt-tab" debugging and echo debugging are "destructive tests". This means that in order to find a problem, you have to change things. This might make it worse, or will endanger your live environment, so both of these methods are not recommended.

Using a Debugger

For proper debugging that doesn't require a code change to investigate a problem, we can use a debugger. There are two major debuggers for PHP:

- Xdebug

- Zend Debugger

The Xdebug extension (`http://www.xdebug.org`) is an open source debugger for PHP which is used by several open source IDEs. The Zend Debugger is used in the Zend IDEs; Studio and Eclipse PDT. Both let you debug a problem on a remote server. Zend Studio also offers the ability to debug a script within Zend Studio itself, without having to connect to the server. This is only useful for relatively small scripts, as for bigger applications, you will want to test it on an actual server.

In a debugger, you can run the code step by step, so line by line you see what is happening in your code. You can set *watches*, which are variables whose value you want to track. You can define *breakpoints* which make the application run up until a certain point. This is useful if you have a bigger application and don't want to start at the first line. A breakpoint is a marker in the code that makes the debugger stop when the application reaches that point in the code.

Most debuggers also feature *conditional breakpoints*. These breakpoints allow you to define an expression that is evaluated to determine if the breakpoint should hold execution. For example, if you have a loop of 10,000 iterations, and you suspect a bug near the final iteration, you could step through the code manually 10,000 times, but you could also define a conditional breakpoint that says break if $i = 9990. This way, the code is looped 9990 times before it breaks, so you only have to step through the final 10 iterations.

Root-Cause Analysis

Probably every developer is familiar with this situation:

```
      Customer: "Hey, this is broken."
  Developer: "What did you do?"
  Customer: "I don't know, I just get this error message."
  Developer: "Hmm, I just tried but it seems to work fine here."
```

This causes a lot of frustration. Developers think it's probably just the user not understanding their application. The users think that nobody wants to help them. In most cases though, the problem is in the communication between the customer and the developer. The bug might be caused by specific circumstances that are hard to reproduce.

There is a tool available that helps in reproducing problems, and it's part of the Zend Platform. What it does is capture the *event context* when something bad happens. What this looks like can be seen in the 7.1.

Whenever an error occurs (a parse error, out of memory error, performance problem or an application specific error) it records all the input data, from the URL

Figure 7.1

($_GET), posted forms ($_POST), server variables ($_SERVER), any cookies that were passed to the script ($_COOKIES) and optionally, anything that was in the session at the time the error occurred ($_SESSION). This makes it easier to reproduce the problem, as it gives you the exact conditions that caused the error to happen.

If you have Zend Studio, you can replay the problem by clicking the *debug* link in the event screen. This will fire up the Zend Debugger so you can debug the issue. What's very helpful here is that the context of the problem is used in the debug session, so you're not just debugging the script; you're debugging the exact situation that caused the problem.

Zend Platform isn't free, but it greatly reduces the time necessary to find a problem, so for business and enterprise environments it is well worth considering.

Source Control

A source control system, or a revision control system or version control system, is a set of tools for managing source code. Before we dive into the details, perhaps we should first answer the question of why we would want our source code to be managed.

Here are a few typical scenarios that developers run into when not yet using a source control system:

- You develop a web site with a team of developers. One of the developers made a change in `somefile.php`. One of the other developers appears to have changed `somefile.php` too. Both were working on different functions but in the same file. Developer A places his version on the test server. Later, Developer B places his version on the test server. Since he wasn't aware of A's changes, he overwrites those, and the application breaks. Even if, in the above scenario, both developers were aware of each others changes, the only way to merge the changes into one file would be to manually copy/paste the changes over.

- You did an update of some files of the application yesterday and now you are confronted with a bug. You wish you could reverse your changes from yesterday. You could restore the backup of the night before your change, but that probably means you lose some of the other changes you did on that day too.

- You develop a new feature for a project but you remember creating something similar a few months ago. You can't remember where that was anymore so you develop it from scratch, again.

- You discover a bug in the software. You have found the line of code that is problematic, but you don't understand why it's there. Probably somebody put it there for a reason. If you change it, you risk breaking something else. But you don't know who created it or why.

- You have fixed a bug in a web site, and it required changes in three separate files. You now want to update the live environment. You have to carefully update the right three files without touching anything else.

- You're working on version 2.0 of your application. Suddenly, a client wants a modification to his installation, but he's still running 1.3. You wish you still had a copy of 1.3 on your development environment. Now you're going to have to copy their environment over before you can make changes.

Most development teams are familiar with at least a few of these scenarios. A source control system is designed to make them a lot easier. It is a repository that not only stores all the code, but also keeps track of all the changes. It keeps a record of who made a change, what they changed, when they changed it, and, by forcing the developer to enter a comment when he makes a change, it also tracks why a change was made.

It doesn't only track those changes, it also allows you to access them. You can reverse changes and you can get older versions of the code-base.

The Process

Using source control on a project starts with importing the project in the source control repository. If you use a source control system from the start, you start out with an empty repository, but if you have an existing application, you can import it into the repository.

Whenever someone needs to work on the application, they "check out" a version of the code-base. Using a command they create a local copy of the source code. Each developer has his own copy. This is important, two developers never work in the same directory but always in their own *sandbox*.

The developers work on the software, and when they finish a change, they *commit* their changes. This adds the changes in the files to the central repository. Each new version of the source is called a *revision*. Usually, a commit requires the developer to enter a small comment which describes their commit, e.g. "added contact form". Other developers 'update' their source, which means that they now have the changes too. By periodically updating and committing, all developers work on the same sources.

If two developers each change the same file, the source control system will automatically merge those changes, so both developers get each others changes without any problem. In the case where the developers changed the same lines (e.g. one developer changed a line to $x=10$ and the other developer changed the exact same line to $x=11$), the source control system doesn't know what to make of it, and will report a *conflict*. It will mark the conflicting code and the developer can resolve it by choosing either of the two versions.

If someone made a mistake and wants to reverse his change, he can revert that change specifically (even if other changes have been committed afterward). This way people can successfully "undo" changes. Even changes from the past.

If you need a specific version of the code, you can tell the source control system you need a specific version and it will check it out for you. This can be based on dates ('give me the code as it was on March the first, last year'), names ('give me the version labeled experimental') or version number ('give me version 1.0.3 of the code').

If you want to see why a certain line of code is the way it is, you can get the history of the file, and see exactly when it was changed, what the commit message was, and who changed it.

The Tools

To use source control, you need a few tools. Generally, source control consists of a server (the repository containing all the code) and a client (the tool that you use to access the repository and to add code to it). There are usually multiple clients to choose from. There are command line clients, which are useful if you need to access the repository via ssh on a server, graphical clients that allow you to easily manipulate the repository, and there are integrated solutions that add source control support to existing applications. Many IDEs have integrated source control, which lets you retrieve code from the repository directly from the IDE. There are also integrations for Windows Explorer, the Mac OSX finder etc., which allow you to easily checkout/commit/update from your file manager. But before you install the tools, you'll have to decide which source control system you are going to use, because there are many to choose from. Here are a few of the more popular ones:

- CVS (Concurrent Versions System) (`http://ximbiot.com/cvs/wiki/`). This is still the most widely adopted source control system. It's been around for years and is supported by a large set of tools. Most IDEs support CVS out of the box. A popular graphical client for windows is TortoiseCVS. It has a few disadvantages though; there is no way to rename a file but to remove it and re-add it with another name; and in this process the history is not preserved. Also, you can't remove directories, and if you need to reverse a commit, you have to do so file by file.

- Subversion or SVN (`http://subversion.tigris.org/`). Subversion is very similar to CVS, but much more modern. It was designed from the start to work like CVS, but without the shortcomings of CVS. Files can be renamed, directories can be (re)moved, and commits are 'atomic', meaning that if you commit three files, you can reverse that in one command, whereas in CVS you would have to reverse each file separately. SVN usage is very similar to CVS though, most commands are exactly the same. This helps people move from CVS to SVN. Subversion is currently the most popular source control system for new projects and adoption is growing rapidly. If you start working with source control, I would recommend to start with SVN right away and not look at CVS. Most modern IDEs support SVN, a popular windows client is TortoiseSVN.

- GIT (`http://git.or.cz/`). GIT is a "distributed" source control system. This means that contrary to CVS and SVN, it doesn't have a central repository. Instead, each developer has his own local repository, and changes are merged from one repository to the other. This is useful for large distributed development projects where there's a hierarchy of people responsible for maintaining the code-base. GIT was developed by Linus Torvalds, author of the Linux Kernel, and the Linux Kernel is one of the most famous projects using GIT for source control.

Personally, for corporate environments I like the central repository approach of CVS and SVN more than the distributed approach, as it means there is a central, controlled, repository that is not dependent on any of the developers. But in some situations a distributed system might be more convenient. SVN and CVS are more common so are probably a safe choice in most situations; if you want to consider distributed source control, I suggest to carefully investigate the characteristics, advantages and disadvantages first.

The aforementioned source control systems are all free software. There are commercial alternatives, but the quality of the free tools is so high that in most situations, these tools will be all you need.

Branches

Once you've mastered the basics of checking out code, updating the code and committing changes, you should have a look at branching. This feature gives you a powerful way to maintain several versions of the software, and to do proper release management.

Branches can best be explained in 7.2

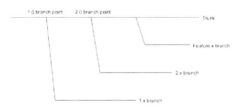

Figure 7.2

The trunk is the main source tree (sometimes called the *main branch*). From the trunk, several branches have sprouted.

A *branch* is a specific version of the software that is maintained separately from the trunk. The trunk contains the latest development, the branches represent previous versions, or versions with specific changes. In each branch, people can make changes.

The way branching works differs slightly from one source control system to the next, but branching is the solution for a number of common scenarios:

- Maintenance on older versions of the software. A bug-fix that is only relevant for version X but not for the current version, can be committed in the version X branch, without interfering with the current code base.

- Development of new features. If a developer plans to develop a feature that has a significant impact on the code base, and doesn't want to risk harming the development of the other team members, he can create his own branch, in which he can develop his features separate from the other developments.

- A managed branch. The trunk usually contains all the changes to the codebase. If you need a version of the software that is more selective, you can create a separate branch and apply only some of the changes from the trunk to that branch.

Tags

Another feature for managing releases is tagging.

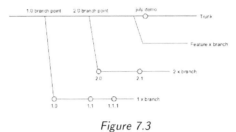

Figure 7.3

The blue dots in 7.3 represent the tags. A tag is a specific release of the software. It is a snapshot in time. A tag cannot be changed[1]. You can tag the software to mark a specific point in time so you can later check out that exact version. A tag could be 'release 1.3.2' or 'the specific version we installed at customer x'.

Merging

Merging is the process of combining changes from one revision into the other. This is useful in the following scenarios:

You have fixed a bug in version 1 of the software, but you also need to apply it to versions 2 and 3. Source control systems allow you to automatically "merge" the software from one branch into the other, so the same changes are applied. This way, you can keep separate versions that are very different, but still selectively apply some changes to all versions. If the code has changed a lot between the two versions, a merge may not always be possible. In this case, the source control system will tell you

---

[1]Depending on the source control system used, this may not be entirely true. In SVN for example, you can theoretically commit in a tag as well, but it's a matter of policy and best practice not to do that. If you need to be able to commit changes in the future, create a branch. If you don't, tag the software. Some source control systems allow you to convert a tag to a branch, but most don't.

that there was a problem merging, and will ask you to apply (some of) the changes manually.

You can *backport* fixes. Backporting is the same process as the previous scenario, but a backport is a change or feature in a newer version that you apply to an older version. This is useful if you fix a security bug in the software and decide that you also want to apply it to older versions.

You have created a separate branch to do some experimental development without endangering the main branch or trunk. When your changes are finished, you merge the changes from this development branch back into the main branch.

Each source control system has its own way to do a merge, consult the documentation for the source control system that you choose for instructions on how to perform a merge.

Issue Tracking

The more projects you run, the more customers you have and the more developers, the bigger the need for issue tracking. In small teams, issues (bugs and feature/change requests) are usually dealt with on an ad hoc basis. Someone reports a bug, and it is either directly fixed, or written down somewhere and dealt with a little later.

In larger projects, it is not always clear who is the best person to solve an issue, because multiple people have worked on it, and the code-base is large. Also, the number of issues can become significantly larger if the project is bigger.

For a project manager, it becomes more difficult to track the status of issues when there are multiple developers.

Issues are often dependent on several factors. For example, a bug may only occur in certain browser versions, or only after a certain sequence of events, or with a certain set of (test-)data. The ad hoc way of dealing with issues often does not cope with these specific issues, and they tend to get lost in the process. To ease the tracking of issues, you can use an issue tracker. Issue trackers generally offer the following functionality:

- The ability to add an issue. Usually consisting of a title, a description, reproduction steps, platform/browser details and version information.

- Assigning issues to developers, so we can see who needs to fix what.

- Tracking the status of an issue. You can see if it is new, if it is assigned to someone, if it is fixed (and when and by whom) and if it is tested.

- Tracking the history of an issue; most issue trackers keep a list of changes, so we can see who changed what and when.

- Planning. Some issue trackers have the ability to set a deadline for an issue, add an estimation of fix time and link issues to specific versions or 'target milestones'. A target milestone can be the release when a fix is planned, e.g. 'this should be fixed before 1.3'. Another important field for issues is the priority. The priority of issues let you distinguish between the things that you should solve right away, as soon as possible or at a later stage.

- Reporting. most trackers have reporting functionality that shows the amount of issues per product, the increase or decrease in number of reported issues over time, fix ratio, fix speed etc.

- Commenting. An issue is not static: people will investigate the issue and collect data. Most issue trackers allow the users to add comments to an issue so the progress can be documented. This is useful if the issue gets reassigned; the new assignee will have all documentation on the issue in one place.

- Access control. Some issue trackers allow fine grained access control to issues. You can grant users access to only certain issues, or issues that meet predefined criteria (such as all issues on a certain product). This is useful if you want to give customers access to your issue tracker. Granting customers access has the advantage that they too can track the progress of the issue, or even add additional information that is useful for the developer. Some feel that communicating about issues through an issue tracker is impersonal; however, information is less likely to get lost if it's in an issue tracker, and an issue tracker does not mean you can't communicate to the customer in person. When used properly, it can improve communication significantly.

- Notification. Issue trackers can email you when issues change. For example, you can request to be emailed when an issue is closed, or when the priority changes.

There are many issue trackers available. Because issue tracking, once you use it, becomes an integral part of your development process, it is important to do a proper evaluation before you settle on a product. Below is a list of popular issue trackers :

- Mantis (`http://www.mantisbt.org/`). Mantis is a popular issue tracker, because it is open source and written in PHP. This makes it easy to customize to your needs. It's easy to install and you're up and running with Mantis very quickly.

- Jira (`http://www.atlassian.com/software/jira/`). Jira is a commercial issue tracker that also features project management features. Its authors classify it as 'enterprise ready'. The Zend Framework project uses Jira as their issue tracker. Jira is written in Java.

- Trac (`http://trac.edgewall.org/`). Trac is a fairly new issue tracker. What makes Trac very interesting is that it integrates with other tools in the software life-cycle. It hooks into SVN to link issues to changes in the software, and comes with an integrated Wiki. Trac is open source and written in Python.

Documentation

We will look at documentation a number of times in this book. In this paragraph, we'll look at some tools that are useful when documenting software.

API Documentation

If you document the source code adhering to the "phpdoc" standard (a standard derived from JavaDoc, but adapted for use in PHP), IDEs can use this documentation to support auto-completion. There are also a number of other tools that you can use to maximize the usefulness of source code documentation:

- phpDocumentor (`http://www.phpdoc.org/`). This tool scans the source code and converts all the phpdoc compliant source code comments into an online reference. This is very useful when there are multiple developers working on a project. Without looking through the code, they can find the documentation of any class or function in the project. An example of the online documentation that phpDocumentor generates is its own online documentation, available at `http://manual.phpdoc.org/HTMLframesConverter/default/`. (This manual is not only useful as an example of what phpDocumentor can do and how it works, it is also an excellent reference for the phpdoc standard).

- PHPXref (`http://phpxref.sourceforge.net/`). PHPXref is similar to phpDocumentor, but is strong in generating cross-references for PHP source code. It analyzes the code and the docblocks, and creates online documentation that makes it easy to navigate through the source, see dependencies within the source and see how functions and classes are used in the project, which file is included where etc.

Wiki

The final tool I want to mention in this chapter is a *wiki*. A wiki is online documentation that can easily be edited. The most well known wiki is Wikipedia (`http://www.wikipedia.org`), the online encyclopedia that can be improved by anyone with an Internet connection.

Wikis can be used to manage internal documentation, but also public documentation. At my company, we employ two wikis. One contains the public documentation that our customers and the users of our open source products can use (and edit!), and one contains all the company specific information. The nice thing about wikis is that the more people get accustomed to them, the more they will want to document in the wiki. Right now, we have anything from company policies to employee benefits, and everything from customer/project information to the architecture of our own web clusters on the wiki.

The main benefit of a wiki over other documentation tools is the ease of use. Documentation in documents tends to rapidly become outdated or get lost. ('I know there's a document with specifications on the file server somewhere, but I don't know what the most recent version is.') Wikis have a special syntax for easily applying markup. For example, some wikis let you surround words with *asterisks* to make them bold, automatically create links from URLs etc.

Cross-linking information is easy as well, which makes wikis very easy to navigate. Most wikis support surrounding a word with [brackets], which will create a hyperlink from the word, linking to a page with exactly that title.

You might wonder if wikis aren't likely to become a mess if anybody can edit anything. The fact that everybody can moderate it usually keeps the wiki clean. In Wikipedia, the sheer number of users makes sure that any abuse or mistake is quickly corrected. In a business environment, you have less users, but also less content, so the overall effect of group moderation will remain, albeit at a slightly smaller scale. And in most wikis, you can keep track of changes to the documentation, and see who made what change and when. This way, moderation of the content is very easy.

To set up a wiki, you need wiki software. There's no need to build this from scratch, as there are many software packages that you can install. Because there are so many, I would like to refer you to `http://en.wikipedia.org/wiki/List_of_wiki_software` for an extensive list.

Chapter 8

Building Blocks

Many applications start with an empty `index.php`, from which the development team starts to work. While there are situations where this may be the best approach, it's usually not necessary to start an application from scratch. In this chapter I will look at software that can be used as a basis when developing applications, and some of the reasoning behind using off the shelf components.

Don't Reinvent the Wheel

When starting a project, you should ask yourself which parts are unique, and which parts are likely to have been developed before? For the parts that have been developed before, you may select software or components. If you perform a proper selection, you may be able to find existing components that fulfill a large part of your development needs.

But be aware that being able to customize the components may be an important requirement. If you need 100 hours to build something from scratch, and 150 hours to customize something that already exists, project managers may be difficult to persuade into choosing the latter. With the right tools however, you can easily save hours when reusing components. In particular, frameworks, which are intended to provide you with mechanisms to easily build your own application, can save an enormous amount of work.

On a regular basis I encounter dialogs like this:

```
"What do you use for logging errors?"
"We built our own logging mechanism."
Or:
"What do you do to get good performance?"
"We created a nifty caching layer."
```

These are examples of typical "wheel" functionality. Everybody has written a caching layer and a logging class at least once. Not reinventing the wheel means realizing that things like caching, logging, database access, sending email and rendering templates are common problems for which excellent solutions exist. Before you build something, have a look at what's out there. It will pay off to start the project with a selection of software, before coding starts.

The "Not Invented Here Syndrome"

If there is so much PHP software out there, how come so much is written from scratch? An important cause is the "Not Invented Here Syndrome". This syndrome consists of a number of reasons that people have for not using existing software. Some of these reasons are valid, but others are not. Let's look at a few reasons.

"The existing software is no good. I can do this better."

This is sometimes a good reason. Most software is not perfect, and many PHP scripts that you find online have dubious quality. Good software selection can help you find the right software for your needs. However, there are 2 pitfalls in this argument. The first is, creating something better from scratch may be more expensive than fixing the existing software. Contributing changes to the existing software may be less time consuming, and just as rewarding. The cost of rewriting something from scratch is often underestimated. Not only do you have to implement much of the same functionality, chances are you will encounter difficulties that the author of the other software has already encountered and overcome before.

The second pitfall is that thinking that you can do better is often not justified. Maybe at this moment you can do a better job because now you are dedicated a good amount of time on it. Maybe you really are a better programmer than the programmers of this particular piece of software, and you do a much better job at it. You really create something beautiful. But after a while, you will be working on other parts of the project. You will no longer dedicate as much time on this component as you initially did. Whereas this other project is still very active. Its authors may be adding new functionality, improving it even further, and after a while, this software may improve in quality and may have more functionality than the 'I can do this better' version.

"The existing software is no good. It can't do Z, but we need Z."

This is a similar argument. Ask yourself how much work it would be to implement X. Check how much work it would be to implement A through Y. Is making something that can do A through Z from scratch less work than taking A through Y and just add Z? Sometimes it is, but it is tempting not to check and to directly rebuild from scratch.

"The existing software is too big. It features A through Z, but we only need A and B."

Software that has too many features can be unnecessarily complex, bloated or even slow. So this can be a very valid argument. Before you try to rewrite, try to look a little bit into the future. Many development projects have started this way, and were very efficient at first because they only implemented A and B, and that was all the developers needed. However as the project grew, there came at a point where they needed C as well, and a few customers later, D through H were required, and after 3 years of development, everything from A through Z had been implemented. It takes a little bit of knowledge about the future to be able to make a decision based on this argument. Still it might be worth-wile to ponder this, since, in the long run, it can make or break a project.

"I know there's existing software, but I like to learn."

It's sometimes true that you learn more from what you build yourself, than from others. This can be a valid argument, but be aware of the consequences in the longer term. Building it yourself, even if there's a viable alternative, means you will also have to maintain it in the long run. You might even learn more from looking at the code from others, and there's plenty to learn from customizing existing software.

"There's existing software but it is not free."

I have often seen people develop a solution because the available off-the-shelf components were not free. Even to the extent where someone built his own JavaScript drop-down menu in 3 days because there was a component that fit the requirements, but it cost 100 dollars. Think about the cost of developing this from scratch in 3 days. There's hardly a manager that can't be convinced to spend some money if it can prevent developers to spend days on developing their own solution.

"But it's fun!"

Work should be fun; you spend roughly half your day on it (if you don't count sleep). But working on new things that somebody else didn't already invent yet ('to boldly go where no one has gone before') can be much more rewarding. Also, for a business, 'fun' should always be in line with 'efficiency'. If something is fun to make but costs a fortune to maintain, it's hard to sell to the boss.

Packages

When you look for existing software components to use as a basis for your developments, have a look at off the shelf software packages. A software package is useful if you are building an application or web site that consists for a large part of common functionality, and that requires only a small level of customization. Let's have a look at a few common scenarios and software packages. (By no means I am able to give a complete overview of packages available, think of this chapter as a pointer in the right direction, but also have a look at other packages offered by the PHP community.)

Content Management

Content Management Systems are probably the most common systems on the Internet. This is not surprising, as almost the entire Internet is made of content. If you're in a project to build a content management system, there are many packages to choose from:

- Joomla (`http://www.joomla.org`)

- ezPublish (`http://www.ez.no`)

- Typo3 (`http://www.typo3.org`)

- Xoops (`http://www.xoops.org`)

All of these are open source, but each has different philosophies, and each have their own strengths and weaknesses. When content management is a major part of your application, evaluate the content management systems available based on the requirements. Note that an off-the-shelf CMS dictates the user-interface of the application: not only the layout, but also the workflow.

Many CMS systems call themselves "Enterprise CMS" systems. Be careful with this designation, as the interpretation varies from application to application. Some use the term Enterprise Content Management because they feel the quality and features are 'enterprise ready', others use the term ECM because they integrate well with existing applications in a business environment. Still others follow the more common interpretation, where ECM is about managing information and document flow in an organization, and improving business processes. There aren't many off-the-shelf PHP content management systems yet that fulfill this definition, but many are rapidly growing in the right direction.

In any case, don't be fooled by the term "enterpris"' that some CMS systems use, but have a look at the requirements and select the CMS that best fits the requirements. (I will look at some more general selection criteria later on in this chapter).

Portals/Communities

Portals and community web sites often revolve around gathering and sharing information. There are some CMS systems that have focused on these areas and as such are more suitable for portals or community sites than others. Here are a few examples:

- Drupal (http://www.drupal.org)

- phpNuke (http://www.phpnuke.org)

E-commerce

If the focus of your project is on e-commerce, have a look at the following PHP packages:

- Magento (http://www.magentocommerce.com)

- ZenCart (http://www.zen-cart.com)

- osCommerce (http://www.oscommerce.com)

Magento is the youngest of the three, but looks very promising; it's written in PHP5 from the start and adheres to modern ideas about web development. ZenCart and osCommerce still have some legacy design considerations, having started in PHP4. On the other hand however, ZenCart and osCommerce have both been around for a long time and have become proven technology. All three are open source.

Forums

A forum (or a "bulletin board" as it used to be called in the early days) is fairly straightforward. Visitors should be able to register for an account, post messages, read messages, reply to messages and that wraps up the core functionality. Additional features include the ability to post attachments, the ability to create user profiles, avatar icons, private messages, moderation and many more.

It is remarkable that, although most forums have similar functionality, there are more than 40 PHP forum packages. For an extensive comparison of forum software, see the wikipedia entry at `http://en.wikipedia.org/wiki/Comparison_of_Internet_forum_software_(PHP)`

Some of the popular ones include:

- phpBB (`http://www.phpbb.com`)

- vBulletin (`http://www.vbulletin.com`)

- FUDforum (`http://fudforum.org`)

phpBB is somewhat controversial because of the amount of security issues that have been found over the years, but is very popular and many customizations can be found. FUDforum is written by Ilia Alshanetsky, a known security expert from the PHP community; if you value security, FUDforum is a good choice. vBulletin is a commercial product but also a popular forum engine.

When selecting a forum, an important factor may be how easy it is to make customizations. Some forum systems feature plugin or module systems, others may not. phpBB employs a modification system that requires manual file edits when installing a modification. If you are going to do a lot of custom development, you may want to look at a more pluggable solution.

Blogs

Blogging is very popular, even in corporate environments. More and more companies have a company blog. Here are two popular blogging platforms written in PHP:

- Wordpress (`http://www.wordpress.org`)

- Serendipity (s9y) (`http://www.s9y.org`)

Both are very easy to extend using a plugin system, and both have a large set of plugins available. Wordpress is more user-friendly, but serendipity is easier to embed into an existing application.

Frameworks

If the level of required customization limits the ability to use standard packages, you can go a level deeper and look at frameworks. Wikipedia describes a framework like this[1]:

"A web application framework is a software framework that is designed to support the development of dynamic web sites, Web applications and Web services. The framework aims to alleviate the overhead associated with common activities used in Web development. For example, many frameworks provide libraries for database access, templating frameworks and session management, and often promote code reuse."

In other words, it helps to prevent reinventing the wheel by providing solutions for common problems and leaves the actual application development up to the development team.

There are many PHP frameworks. Since 2006, when the use of frameworks became very popular, there has been a giant increase in the number of frameworks; even framework developers often seem to suffer from the Not Invented Here Syndrome. I have tried to categorize them into a few main categories, but there is some overlap, so don't be offended if you think I put a framework in the wrong category.

---

[1] `http://en.wikipedia.org/wiki/Web_application_framework`

Component Frameworks

Component frameworks are the oldest type of framework in the PHP world. They provide components or classes that solve a particular problem. They're like a Swiss pocket knife. In general, they don't prescribe how an application should be built. If you need to import RSS feeds, you take an RSS component, if you need a basic MVC layer, you use some Model, View and Controller base-classes that they provide. You use what's useful and you don't use what you don't like. The Zend Framework calls this a "Use At Will architecture", but it's a common characteristic of component frameworks. Because of this, it's possible to mix component frameworks with other software or frameworks.

Here are a few examples of component frameworks:

- PEAR (`http://pear.php.net`)

- ezComponents (`http://ez.no/ezcomponents`)

- Zend Framework (`http://framework.zend.com`)

PEAR, the "PHP Extension and Application Repository", is probably the oldest component framework. Ever since PHP has become popular, PEAR was around with useful components and scripts that solve common problems.

Both ezComponents and Zend Framework present themselves as "enterprise ready". Both offer a wide range of components, but what makes them ready for the enterprise is not so much the components they offer, but the process involved in developing them. Both have a well thought out development process centered around proposing ideas, reviewing them, designing a solution and implementing it. Both use automated unit tests to guard quality and compatibility.

Also, there is a big focus on process and quality. This is a very good thing when relying on components from these frameworks in a business critical application. Both frameworks seem to have a good level of maturity. The Zend Framework has a few arguable advantages such as a big base of contributors, the fact that Zend is behind it, and the integration Zend provides with other tools such as Zend Studio and Zend Platform. ezComponents on the other hand, builds on many years of experience of the ezPublish crew, and has a strong leader, Derick Rethans, a highly regarded, well known developer in the PHP community.

Full Stack Frameworks

There are a number of frameworks that go beyond providing components. They lay the groundwork of the application and prescribe the way you develop the application. If component frameworks are Swiss army knives, these so-called *full stack* frameworks are the steel frames that buildings are build from.

Some examples of full stack frameworks:

- CakePHP (`http://www.cakephp.org`)

- Symfony (`http://www.symfony-project.org`)

CakePHP was modeled after the popular Ruby on Rails framework for the Ruby language. It is not a strict port but applies some of the useful concepts from Rails to a PHP framework.

What makes Symfony interesting is that they not only encourage concepts such as "Don't reinvent the wheel," but also adhere to this rule themselves. Instead of building everything from scratch, they have selected a few existing components to build the framework on. You will find that the Propel ORM library is part of Symfony, internationalization is reused from the Prado framework, and many other components have been integrated into the Symfony code. Ironically, many other frameworks preach the "Don't reinvent the wheel" philosophy but then implement everything from scratch.

When using a full stack framework, make a careful selection, as the framework will dictate how you are going to build the application. Each framework may also have some requirements. Symfony for example needs command line access because it has some command line scripts that you need to run.

JavaScript Frameworks

PHP applications often don't consist of just PHP code. The client side is just as important. More and more applications have rich clients, using JavaScript and Ajax to enhance the usability of the application. You can write JavaScript and Ajax code from scratch, directly working with obscure JavaScript elements such as `XmlHttpRequest`, but if you want to save time and build on what others already have done, use a JavaScript framework. Here are a few examples of JavaScript frameworks:

- Prototype (http://prototypejs.org)

- jQuery (http://jquery.com)

- Script.aculo.us (http://script.aculo.us)

- Yahoo YUI (http://developer.yahoo.com/yui)

- Dojo (http://www.dojotoolkit.org)

Prototype is a powerful enhancement to JavaScript. It tries to make JavaScript more 'OOP' friendly, adds some very useful shortcuts, such as:

```
// instead of document.getElementById('element')
$('element')
// instead of document.getElementById('name').value
$F('name')
// instead of a cumbersome XmlHttpRequest implementation
new Ajax.Request('/some_url', { method:'get' })
```

jQuery is similar, it features enhancements to JavaScript to make life easier.

Script.aculo.us is a library that builds on top of prototype, and provides user interface functionality, such as widgets, animations, drag and drop functionality. Both YUI and Dojo are user interface toolkits, that allow you to build a rich web interface by providing widgets, controls and guidelines on how to create solid JavaScript applications.

Like Symfony, dojo also adhered to "Don't reinvent the wheel"; it used several existing JavaScript libraries as its basis.

JavaScript frameworks are independent from the language that is being used on the server side. Although the syntax of Prototype resembles constructs from the Ruby language, it can easily be used in a PHP application.

One word of caution when using JavaScript frameworks: it's easy to get lost in the eye-candy they provide. Use them wisely: don't add visual gimmicks because you can, or because they look cool; do use them when they enhance the user experience and the usability of your application.

Special Purpose Frameworks

Beside the frameworks mentioned above, that are more or less general purpose, there is a set of frameworks that try not to build a complete solution but focus on a particular need, or a particular type of application.

One powerful framework that tries not to be a full stack framework but just to provide an MVC implementation for PHP applications is CodeIgniter (`http://codeigniter.com`). CodeIgniter is fairly lightweight, because it sticks to its core business, which is to provide an MVC implementation.

Another special purpose framework is Propel (`http://propel.phpdb.org`). Propel is a framework that provides an Object Relational Mapping (ORM). For those that skipped chapter 6, an ORM deals with the problem of mapping an object model to a relational database. Propel provides a framework that solves the ORM problem for the developer.

As a last example, I'm shamelessly abusing my power as author of this book to promote a framework that I've been working on for quite a few years now, the ATK framework (`http://www.atk-framework.com`). ATK is a *business framework*, as it focuses only on business applications. It provides a toolkit that allows creation of data management applications, custom CMS back-ends with as little code as possible. This (full stack) framework is useful in business environments and is usually used for internal applications (human resources, resource planning, data management).

Libraries and Components

Originally, a library was a set of useful utilities or components, and a framework was something you built an entire application with. Given the popularity of frameworks however, most libraries now call themselves frameworks, and what used to be a framework is now called a full-stack framework. Still, there are many libraries and components that are useful when developing applications. Need to export to Microsoft Excel? There are numerous libraries that can create Excel files in PHP. Need to generate images? Check out PHP's GD and Imagick extensions. A template engine? Try Smarty.

There are so many that it would not make much sense to provide a list here. Some general advice on where to find useful libraries:

- PHP extensions (`http://www.php.net/extensions`)

- PECL (PHP Extension Community Library, `http://pecl.php.net`)

- Wikipedia (`http://en.wikipedia.org/wiki/List_of_PHP_libraries`)

- Google; just search for 'php' and whatever you need a library for

- Hotscripts (`http://www.hotscripts.com/PHP/Scripts_and_Programs/index.html`) (or any of its many competitors)

Software Selection

There are a few general criteria you should evaluate when selecting software, regardless of whether it's a blog, a forum, a CMS or some library. Of course you should first check if it meets your requirements, but also have a look at the other criteria listed below.

Documentation

Software is only as good at its documentation. Though there exist components that are so intuitive to use that documentation would be overkill, for the majority of software, documentation is essential. Look for API documentation, code documentation, and preferably manuals and tutorials. When you are going to have to customize the software, some documentation on the inner workings of the software would be useful too, in addition to code documentation.

Licensing

Take a good look at the license of the software you plan to use, and whether it's compatible with your use of the software. If you are going to distribute software in a closed source fashion, there are libraries that don't allow this scenario. There are many different licenses and conditions to the use of software, and you should be careful not to violate the terms of the software you use.

Note that when developing a PHP application, you are not limited to open source licenses. This may sound obvious, but I know from experience that many developers tend to look at free software first and stop there. If there is a commercial software package that costs money, developers sometimes stay away from it. From a business point of view however, this is not always the right thing to do: as we already discussed when we talked about the "Not Invented Here" syndrome, there are many occasions where buying a piece of software for, say, $500 is worth double its license cost, if it saves the development team from reinventing the same wheel.

Support

Check the support that is available for a component. Usually there is some form of support from either the developers or the community. If however, a component is business critical for you, you may consider some form of commercial support, where you have a guarantee that someone will help you in case of trouble. Often, with popular software that has a large community, the community support is sufficient for your everyday needs, but there's no guarantee that someone helps you within a certain amount of time. Most software components offer extensive support programs to tackle this, and by paying for such services, you often also help the development of the software.

Code Quality

Code Quality is often an important criteria. If the software is used as a black box, and does its job well, you may not have to know if it's spaghetti code on the inside. However, if you're going to have to change or customize the code, code quality is important. The easier it is to understand the code, the easier it is to customize. Complex, hard to understand magic will frustrate developers and consume a lot of time.

Vitality

The *vitality* of a software component indicates if a project is actively developed. If you're going to use a software component but the latest version is from 2002, it is probably not up to date with the latest versions of PHP and the latest standards in security. It's also harder to get support on a project that has been silent for a while. Indicators are the release frequency of updates, and the activity in the community of a software component.

Customization

I would like to spend a few words on customization of standard software. If you take some rules of thumb into account, you'll have more benefit from your customizations. A common scenario when reusing and customizing software is the following: you incorporate the software, make some customizations, and you're finished. This works fine, but after a while, the software you use will have released new versions, and you'll run into upgrade issues. Let's look at a few methods to avoid these issues.

Get in Touch

Before you start customizing, check with the authors of a product or a the community. Somebody may have already developed the changes you are planning to make. There might be a development version that is newer than the latest stable release you're using, and it may already contain some of the changes you need. It would be a waste of time if you would spend a few days customizing the software, only to find out that somebody already made the same changes. If there's a community, check there to see if somebody is already working on your features, or contact the authors directly.

Externalize

When you make changes, try to keep them out of the original code base as much as possible. Instead of hacking the base code, create plugins. This doesn't guarantee that your code will continue to work without changes when you update the external software, but it does reduce the chance things will break, and it will also make it easier to upgrade the software.

Not all software allows you to make changes without touching the code base. But many applications, usually the ones that have been around for a while, have a plugin or module system that allows you to hook into the software without touching its internals.

Patch

If you can't put your modifications in separate files, you will have to modify the code of the external software that you are using. You are going to want to upgrade the software at some point, so it's important to find a way to make your changes and still be able to upgrade. A simple way is to mark your changes with documentation, as such:

```
// HACK; changed 10 to 50 here because we need a longer timeout
```

This way, when upgrading, you just have to look for the HACK markers and re-apply your changes to the new version.

A slightly more sophisticated way is to create a *patch file*. Using the diff command, you can create a file that contains the differences between your version of the software and the original version, as such:

```
diff -Naur wordpress/ wordpress_original/ > patchfile
```

This file can now automatically be applied to a new version using the patch command:

```
patch -p1 < patchfile
```

If the software changed in such a way that the patch file can't automatically be applied, it will tell you which parts succeeded and which parts failed. For an explanation of the parameters used (and to check which ones are appropriate in your case), see the manuals of the diff and patch commands.

You can keep track of your patches by storing them along with your code in a repository such as SVN.

Contribute

The best way to keep external software upgradable and to reduce the chance of future incompatibilities, is to contribute the changes you made back to the project. If they accept your changes and make them part of the software, then when you upgrade to the next version, your changes will still be present. This does require a little extra effort: you will have to make sure your changes are acceptable by the project, and useful for the general public. This sometimes means you have to make it slightly more generic than when you would have just changed something for your own good.

Chapter 9

Security

Security is an important aspect of application development. The chapter on security is positioned in this book even before we talk about coding, because security is not something you can easily add to an application later; it's not a feature. It's something every developer needs to take into account when writing code. There are entire books on security, and in the last paragraph of the chapter I will recommend several books. This chapter discusses some of the basics.

Don't Trust Input

One of the basic concepts of security in applications is to never trust any input. Whether it be user input, input from external sources, cookies sent to your application or variables in the URL, anything from the outside world can potentially harm your application.

A classic example of what can happen when input is not validated is SQL injection. Consider the following query:

```
mysqli_query("DELETE FROM order WHERE id=$id");
```

if $id is retrieved from the URL (for example, delete.php?id=3), consider what would happen if someone would request the following URL:

```
delete.php?id=id
```

In this case, the literal value "id" is inserted into the query, and the following query is sent to your database:

```
DELETE FROM order WHERE id=id
```

The WHERE clause of the query is true for all records in the database, and the entire table will be emptied.

The solutions to this type of attack are usually easy; in this case, checking whether $id is actually a number would have solved the problem. What validation needs to be done depends on the particular situation.

The best way to prevent problems with input is to identify all inputs to the application, and take appropriate measures for each of them. Make input filtering an integral part of the application (as opposed to validating each and every variable individually when it is used), so it is clear for all developers how input is handled and there is less risk for individual developers to make mistakes.

Escape Where Necessary

Not trusting input is an important aspect of keeping an application secure. However, we should not only look at what others enter into our application, but also how we are handling the data.

Output

Every application has output. Naturally, most web applications output HTML, often combined with JavaScript. To make sure the output is displayed properly and securely, output needs to be escaped before it is sent to the browser.

The next example outputs a product name as an "alt-tag" for an image:

```
$filename = 'penguin.jpg';
$alt = '17" plush penguin';
echo '<img src="'.$filename.'" alt="'.$alt.'">';
```

This code will generate invalid HTML:

```
<img src="penguin.jpg" alt="17" plush penguin">
```

In this case, the result is wrong, but relatively harmless, but there are many situations, where there are security risks, such as in the case where JavaScript is injected.

The solution is to escape the output; in this particular case, the PHP function htmlspecialchars can be used. Depending on the situation, there are other ways to escape the output.

Queries

With queries the same problem could occur, in particular with single and double quotes. What `htmlspecialchars` does for HTML output, `mysql_real_escape_string` does for SQL queries. (For other databases, there are similar functions). It escapes the data using the method that is prescribed by the database vendor.

Don't be tempted to use `addslashes`. Using `addslashes` transforms " to \ " and although this seems to work for MySQL, and seems to be an easy way to escape quotes, `addslashes` is not intended for database escapes. It gives a false sense of security, and in some databases, it has the effect that the \ character will be stored in the database.

Escape Considerations

An important consideration is where to escape the data. You can escape data before it is stored in the database, so the database contains already escaped data and can safely be output, or you can escape data after it is retrieved from the database. From a performance point of view, the first way may be more efficient: you escape once before you save data to the database, and when that data is retrieved many times, you have saved many calls to the escape functions.

However, there are several disadvantages to this approach. One is that the data in the database becomes specific to one type of output. Escaping is different depending on the output medium. For HTML, you escape differently than you would for JavaScript. Similarly if you use the data in the database also for PDF output, desktop applications, reports or other media, escaping is different again. Another disadvantage is that people may rely on the data being escaped before it is saved, and if new code is written or a new application is used, which does not escape the data, you will run into security problems. Furthermore, the overhead of escaping the data after being retrieved from the database is very small compared to actually reading the data from the database. If performance of escaping does become an issue, it's still better to apply caching techniques than to change the way data is being escaped.

Authentication

Code security is important, but security encompasses more than just that. Another area of security is authentication. There are a number of ways to handle authentication, and in professional applications, you may need to take into account whether there are already other applications that require authentication. If there are, you may want to hook into the authentication of those applications so users can have a single account for all applications within a business. The best way to hook into different types of authentication is to abstract the authentication into a set of classes that each handle authentication in their own specific way; one that can authenticate against a database, one that authenticates against an apache .htaccess file, LDAP, Active Directory, etc. If the interface is consistent, it's easy to switch authentication methods if necessary. If you use a framework, there may already be an authentication mechanism that you can use; many frameworks support various types of authentication. Regardless of how you implement it, it's best to assume that your application is not going to be the only application, so keep authentication loosely coupled to the application.

OpenID

Business applications are not the only applications that require authentication. More and more web sites offer functionality that requires an account: social networks like Facebook and LinkedIn, sites like YouTube or Flickr, and forums. Even plain old search engines offer additional benefits if the visitor creates an account, such as Google's iGoogle interface[1]

---

[1] iGoogle can be accessed via http://www.google.com/ig.

One effect of this trend is that users have an enormous collection of accounts and are very likely to either forget their passwords a lot, or use the same credentials on many different sites. This poses some serious security risks.

If you build a web site that requires authentication, consider implementing OpenID (`http://openid.net/`). OpenID is a generic authentication service that allows users to identify themselves to many different sites using a single identity. It is increasing in popularity rapidly, as more and more web sites realize that forcing visitors to create yet another account is going to be problematic in the long run.

At this moment however, OpenID isn't common enough to rely on it as the only authentication method on a web site. If you want to provide OpenID authentication, also add different ways to authenticate people. This will require a little extra effort, but will help promote OpenID, and in the long term will make it easier not only for web site visitors, but also for web site developers.

Authorization

Authentication deals with granting a user access to an application; it is used to verify someone's identity. The second step is authorization: checking what a user is allowed to do. Authorization may be very high level, granting access to a certain part of an application to a user, or very low level, by controlling access to every detailed feature. With fine grained access control, a user could be able to see data but not modify it, or modify it but not delete it.

The requirements of the application should determine how fine grained access control should be. If low level access control is not necessary, don't add it; administrators will get annoyed by the amount of privileges they have to assign to users.

Determining what functions to grant access to is only half of the authorization of an application. Who to give them to is the other half. Most applications use one of the following ways to grant privileges :

- User-based; each user has its own set of privileges. This is a useful scheme when there aren't a lot of users, or when each user has a completely different set of privileges.

- Group-based; users belong to one or more groups and each group has a set of privileges. The privileges that a user has is the complete set of privileges assigned to each of the groups he belongs to. This scheme is useful if there are many users and the users can logically be divided into groups. In business applications, groups could be linked to departments or teams, or to people with a certain function, such as developers or managers.

- Role-based; technically role-based authorization is exactly the same as group-based authorization. We speak of roles instead of groups if we can identify specific roles that a person can play in an organization. Roles are often linked to certain tasks. Examples of roles are "article editor," "quality control," "architect," or "project administration." Roles are slightly more fine-grained than groups, and are useful when roles change a lot. If someone is out of the office for a while, he may assign some of his tasks to several different coworkers. By adding the roles these people play to their account, they now have the rights to perform the tasks of the person they are covering for.

- Level-based; if privileges are purely hierarchical, creating security levels is an option. This (rather uncommon) approach defines a set of levels, and the privileges that someone with a certain level has. For example, most users may have level 0, project managers have level 1 and company management has level 2. Each level increases the number of privileges a person has. Someone with level 3 has all the privileges that belong to level 3, plus all the privileges of the lower levels. The reason this scheme isn't very common is that it is often hard to define a purely hierarchical structure. Some people may be considered "lower" in rank than other people, but still they might need to perform some tasks that require privileges normally attributed only to higher-level staff.

Sometimes it may be necessary to use a combination of the above. A practical example would be an application that has group access rights, but also allows additional privileges to be defined for individual users. Note that this adds an extra level of complexity; the simpler you can keep this, the less likely you are to introduce security problems.

The set of privileges assigned to a user, group, role or level is called an *Access Control List* or ACL.

The safest way to deal with access control is to use a white-list approach. This means that nobody has access to a certain feature unless explicitly granted. The black-list approach would be to grant everybody access, unless specifically denied. White-listing is safer than black-listing, since if things go wrong, or the ACL is not properly configured or malfunctioning, at least you are not granting access to areas of an application that should not be open to the public.

A Secure Infrastructure

Securing an application does not guarantee a secure environment. Every component in a system can be vulnerable to security holes. The following measures can help maintain a secure environment.

- Create a list of all software packages used by the system (from the operating system to any third party library used), and make sure you track security announcements for all the components. If a security issue was found and a solution exists, apply it.

- Close any port that you are not using. For example, if your application does not use FTP, do not run an FTP server.

- Grant access only to people who need it.

- Use personal accounts (no generic accounts used by the entire company which makes it hard to track down security issues).

- Use only secured access to an environment. SSH instead of telnet, scp or sFTP instead of FTP. Use SSL encryption for any page that contains private data and any page that private data is sent to. (This may not be limited to check-out pages in a web-shop, but sometimes back-end applications need to be secured too).

- Avoid having to grant people root access; if configured properly, people that need access to the system can do what they need to do with their own account.

- "Security by obscurity" isn't the best form of security, but it's an additional barrier. (A painting in front of a safe doesn't mean you can leave the safe open; still it's an additional level of security). For PHP applications this means that you don't expose what you don't need to. People do not need to know what version of Apache, PHP etc. you run, so you can turn off those options in your configuration files. If you use the Zend debugger component on the server, tell it to not expose it remotely so people will not try to debug it.

This is not an extensive list; these are just a few examples that can help you keep an environment secure. The books in the next section are strongly recommended if you want to create a secure application.

Book Recommendations

I have found the following 2 books on security to be informative and practical. They are both written by security experts from the PHP community:

- "Essential PHP Security" by Chris Shiflett[2]

- "php|architect's Guide to PHP Security" by Ilia Alshanetsky[3]

---

[2] http://www.oreilly.com/catalog/phpsec/
[3] http://phparch.com/c/books/id/0973862106

Chapter 10

Development

So, let's imagine we are in a kitchen. We know what we're going to cook, we've got the recipe, the ingredients and the kitchen is ready. All that's left is following the recipe to make our meal. In other words, we are prepared and ready to develop our application. You will find that this chapter is relatively short. The actual development of an application is rather straightforward once we are properly prepared. Of course, there is a lot to learn about PHP programming, but there are many different books and other resources that can teach you to program. Most of you reading this book are probably already developing in PHP and are just looking for ways to professionalize. So in this chapter, I want to cover just a few programming related topics that haven't been covered in the previous chapters.

Code Structure

When writing code, keep it structured. A PHP application does not contain just PHP code, but a mix of HTML, PHP, CSS and JavaScript. One way to deal with this myriad of languages without getting lost along the way is to keep them properly separated.

- Put HTML in template files. Whether you are using a template engine like Smarty, or using PHP itself as a template language; place the HTML code in a separate file.

- Place layout in CSS files. Resist the temptation to use inline styles (`<div style="...">`), as this reduces the maintainability of the layout. Even though the M in HTML is for "markup," and was originally intended to contain the layout of a web site, nowadays it is much better to keep the HTML layout-free. The HTML should only contain the structure and semantics of the web pages. Use the proper HTML tags to define the meaning of content; `H1` for titles, `P` for paragraphs, and so on.

- JavaScript belongs in JavaScript files. While it may seem convenient to be able to mix scripts with HTML (e.g. defining an onclick event on an element), it is better to do this in a separate `.js` file. This will keep the HTML clean and the scripts will be easier to develop and maintain. Note however that registering event handlers on elements can be tricky, as different browsers have different ways of dealing with this. The JavaScript libraries mentioned a few chapters earlier can help deal with this while avoiding cross-browser hassle.

- Finally, the PHP code goes into PHP files. Don't put everything in one big file, but create a directory structure with logical directories that contain the code. If you have a modular approach, create a directory per module. A common practice is to use a separate file per class, so there should never be more than one class in a file, and developers should be able to derive the location of a class from its name. A proper directory and file structure eases navigation through the code base.

Don't Repeat Yourself

One of the most useful principles during development is the "Don't Repeat Yourself" or DRY principle. This principle states that everything you do, you should only do once. In essence, this means that copy/paste is taboo.

If you feel you have to use the same piece of code elsewhere in the application, put the code into a function or utility class that you can use in both places. This helps reduce the amount of code you write. The less code you write, the less code you have to maintain, and the higher the quality of the software. (This by the way, is why it's bad to measure a programmer's productivity by looking at the amount of code he writes; a good programmer often removes more code than he adds, except for at the start of a project of course.)

Refactoring

Often the code that you need twice is not exactly the same in both situations; it should behave slightly differently. Again, this is no reason to copy/paste and then change the code. The proper solution is *refactoring*. This means that you take the original code and change it in such a way that it meets the requirements of both situations. Sometimes this means moving it to a function and adding parameters that influence its behavior. Sometimes it means extending a class and overriding a few of its methods to change its behavior.

Consistency

The DRY principle has an additional advantage: it makes it easier to create a consistent application. This is best explained with an example. Suppose you have a TextEditor widget with the following API:

```
class TextEditor
{
  public function __construct($name)

  /**
   * Set the width in characters.
   */
  public function setWidth($width)
  {
     ....
  }

  /**
   * Set the height in number of lines
   */
  public function setHeight($height)
  {
     ....
  }

  /**
```

```
 * If set to true, the text will be wrapped at word boundaries.
 */
public function setWrap($wrap)
{
  ....
}

/**
 * Render the TextEditor as HTML code
 */
public function render()
{
  ....
}

}
```

When you use this `TextEditor` somewhere in the application, you could for example use it like this:

```
$editor = new TextEditor('description');
$editor->setHeight(20);
$editor->setWidth(80);
$editor->setWrap(true);
echo $editor->render();
```

You can place this code everywhere you need a TextEditor, but then you'll be repeating code; this violates the DRY principle. Setting the height and width in several different places will sooner or later lead to differences. In some part of the application the height will be changed, and things become inconsistent. For an application, it's better to refactor this in such a way that we achieve consistency throughout the application, while minimizing code. In this example, we could solve this by creating a specialization for use throughout the application:

```
class MyappTextEditor extends TextEditor
{
  public function __construct($name)
  {
    parent::__construct($name);
    $this->setHeight(20);
    $this->setWidth(80);
```

```
    $this->setWrap(true);
  }
}
```

If the application now uses the `MyappTextEditor` class instead of the `TextEditor` class, we are sure that it looks the same in all situations it is used. We might even make it more flexible by moving the constants into a configuration file so that we can easily change settings like this without having to change the classes.

In the case where we do need a text editor that looks different, we can still use the original `TextEditor` instead of `MyappTextEditor`.

Documentation

It is important to document code. This improves maintainability and ensures that you still know how the code works when you look at it years after it was developed.

phpdoc

In the *Tools* chapter, we looked at some useful tools for generating online documentation based on comments in the code. All of these tools work with the phpdoc standard. Let's look at an example PHP file with phpdoc comments. This gives an impression of the phpdoc standard (which is very straightforward so it shouldn't take much time to get used to), and a short explanation of what to write in the comments.

```php
<?php

/**
 * File header; explain the purpose and general contents of the
 * file.
 *
 * @package If the app is divided into modules or packages, you
 *          can define a package and @subpackage here. The tools
 *          that convert the comments to API documentation use
 *          this to create documentation per package.
 *
 * @copyright (c) 2008 Company-name
 * @license This file is licensed under the ... license
 */
```

```
/**
 * Short description.
 *
 * Longer description; describe the purpose of the class. What
 * it can be used for, what functionality it provides.
 *
 * @author The author of the class. (This may seem redundant if
 *         you use a source control system like SVN, but not
 *         everybody will look at the code via SVN, so it is
 *         useful to document who they can contact in case of
 *         questions.)
 */
class HelloWorld
{
  /**
   * Explanation of a member variable
   */
  private $_someVar;

  /**
   * Explanation of the purpose of a member function.
   * @param String $someParameter Explanation of the parameter.
   * @return Boolean Explanation of the return value.
   */
  public function someFunction($someParameter)
  {
    return true;
  }
}
?>
```

All elements that start with @ are tags that give meaning to the documentation. The documentation tools covered in the *Tools* chapter parse the source code, extract the comments, process these tags and generate structured documentation. The above example only contains the most common tags. There are many additional useful tags that can be found in the phpDocumentor documentation (http://manual.phpdoc.org/)

Inline Comments

The code itself (the bodies of functions and methods) should also be documented. But pay attention to what you write in the comments; don't comment because you need to comment, but write only useful comments. Take the following comment:

```
// Loop through the array of titles
foreach ($titles as $title)
```

This is an example of comments that aren't really useful. The code is clear, and there's no need to explain what the code is doing. Code that is well written documents itself; it is readable and understandable.

The following is an example of useful comments:

```
// We load the data from the database at this point only because
// earlier we lacked the keys to retrieve it, and retrieving it
// any later than this would lead to an inefficiency in WhatEver.
$records = $db->select($where);
```

This time, the comment does not explain what the code is doing or how it is doing it (that should always be clear from the code), but why it is doing it this way or at this moment. In other words, the comments are used to explain things that are not clear from the code itself; the reasoning behind the code. This type of documentation will be needed if other people work with this code or if you look at the code years after you have written it.

Coding Standards

Code readability is improved if the style of the code is consistent throughout an application. In particular when many developers are working on the same project, the code is easier to read if all developers follow the same set of rules. In order to enforce this, you should define coding standards. You can define your own, or you can use an existing set of standards. The advantage of using an existing one is that all arguments for doing something one way or the other have already been weighed. Another advantage is that if you use the standards of a well-known project, chances are that developers are already familiar with them and can more easily adjust to writing in the prescribed style.

If you use a pre-built software package or a framework, the easiest solution is to adhere to the standards used in that project.

When writing something from scratch, you can still look at other software to define standards. Here are some examples of PHP coding standards:

- Zend Framework (`http://framework.zend.com/manual/en/coding-standard.html`)

- PEAR (`http://pear.php.net/manual/en/standards.php`)

Chapter 11

Quality Assurance

As cliché as it sounds: nobody is perfect. We all make mistakes. Development is a complex task with many factors. On every step of the way between an idea and the end result, there is room for error. It's important to test an application before it is put in production to reduce the number of bugs to a minimum. There are several areas that require testing, and there are several ways to do it. We will examine them in this chapter.

Developer Testing

Let's start with the most obvious test mechanism. The developers can test their code after they have written it. Coding is a delicate process, mistakes are easily made (a tiny typo can easily have a huge impact), so it is a good thing for developers to test their code after they have written it.

The advantage of having a developer test his own code is that he knows how the code works and can identify areas that are complex and susceptible to errors. It is important to realize however that this is also a significant disadvantage.

One reason is that it's scary to test your own code. You've been working on a solution for a very complex problem for days; it was a difficult accomplishment and after hours and hours of hard labor you finally have a solution that works in all scenario's that you've envisioned. The relief of finally being done with it does not motivate to put it to a thorough test that might reveal flaws that will take hours and hours more to fix. This has nothing to do with the personality of the developer, this is just human nature.

The second reason why developers testing their own code is problematic, is the frame of reference that the developers are working from. Errors are not only caused by typos, but can also be caused by misinterpretations of the specification, or by wrong assumptions. If a developer tests the result of his own work, chances are that the same misinterpretations or assumptions are still present during the test. For example, if a developer does not take into account that a user could enter negative amounts in his shopping cart, and fails to programmatically validate the number, there's a big chance that when he tests his shopping cart software, he doesn't think of trying to order 'minus 10 copies' either. (I have seen custom e-commerce solutions where I could order negative amounts of stuff and have my shopping cart tell me that I would actually receive money when placing the order).

A good way to improve the quality of developer testing is to have developers test each others code. This way they are not 'blinded' in the way that developers are when they test their own code as we've seen above. A requirement for this approach is that even the developers that test, have knowledge about the code that was written. This is however a good idea anyway as it also increases the ability of developers to help each other, or to take over in case a developer falls ill. Be careful though that there are some negative aspects to testing each others code. It can increase competition and might also lead to frustration between developers at times. It is the responsibility of the entire team, and the project/development manager in particular, to make sure this doesn't happen. In the end, it increases the quality of the end result which is good for the team as a whole.

The ideal way to test is to have a mix of the methods described above: have developers testing both their own code, and each others'. This will combine the advantages of the two methods and will minimize their disadvantages.

Project managers should make sure that testing is taken into account at the planning stage. It is usually the responsibility of developers to estimate the amount of time it takes to develop a certain feature, but both developers and project managers need to make sure that testing is part of the estimates and part of the project plan.

Functional Testing

The shopping cart example of the previous section is perhaps fairly obvious. Often these validations are covered in the functional specifications (this will depend on the level of detail of the specification), but functionality is usually more subtle and may require knowledge of the subject that an application covers. Often the development team members are not experts in the domain the software is intended for. What may be obvious to the business analyst who wrote the specification for a stock market exchange web site, will not be obvious for the development team that takes on the job of developing this web site.

This is why it's important to incorporate functional tests. Functional tests, as the name already implies, test the functionality of an application, and can be performed by people who have knowledge about the desired functionality and the subject of the application. Ideally, this group includes (some of) the users of the system.

A traditional approach to development is to receive specifications from a customer, then develop the product, and in the end, deliver it to the customer. More often than not, the customer will find issues that your development team has not taken into account. To improve the end result it is a good thing to have the customer participate in the functional tests of the application. It is easy to explain to a customer that his knowledge on the subject is essential to the success of the project, and usually customers like being involved in the project even in the early stages. It even increases the customer's tolerance for errors: a bug in an application that the users have helped testing will be perceived differently than the same bug in an application that the customer was not involved in. Again for the project manager, it is important to realize that functional testing takes time. It takes time to run the test, but also time to fix issues that will be found. In particular if the customer is involved, it is important to plan the functional tests, as project progress will depend on the availability of both the development team and the customer.

Functional testing is not only useful to uncover errors in the functionality, it can also help improve the usability of an application. In web applications, usability is influenced by a number of factors including the position of elements on screen, the amount of clicks it takes to execute a certain task, and the overall ease of use of the application. A development team, which typically consists of people with a technical background will have different views on usability from the end user, which is another reason to have the end user test the application at an early stage. This can be as early as the specification phase, by going over wireframe documents with the customer or the users, but it's also useful to have users test the application during or after development.

Environmental Testing

Functionality is only one of the areas of a development project where things may go wrong. The environment of an application is another factor to take into account. The environment of a PHP application consists of two major items: the server on which the application runs, and the browser that the end users or visitors use.

Server Environment

The servers that an application will eventually run on are almost never exactly equal to the environment that the development team has been using. It is important to mimic the eventual environment as much as possible. If it is not possible to make the development environment equal to the production environment (for example when every developer runs a local PHP stack on his workstation), try to mimic the live server as close as possible. It is also important to have a final test on the actual environment before a site goes live.

This is important because subtle differences between the environments can break an application. The following items are examples of differences that can cause trouble:

- PHP version (even differences in minor version numbers)

- PHP settings

- Web server settings

- Database configuration

- Architecture (for example a cluster versus a standalone machine)

- Operating System

- Used libraries (for example the external libraries that PHP extensions such as SimpleXML or CURL use)

The list goes on. Because of the amount of components involved it can be hard to keep environments similar, which is why a test environment on the actual environment is a good idea. I will cover environments in more detail in Chapter 13 (*Deployment*). For this chapter, just remember that it's important to test with the situation that you will have in the live environment. Nothing is more frustrating than having an application developed that relies heavily on an external library, only to discover that once you go live, it appears to be incompatible with the version of the library on the live environment.

Client Environment

Another environment aspect is the browser that the end user is using. This usually is a mix of Firefox, Internet Explorer, Safari, Opera, etc. (Feel free to e-mail me with "hey, you didn't name browser x!" comments but you get my point; there are many different browsers). Even if all users were using the same browser, there are many different browser versions (Firefox 1, Firefox 2, IE6, IE7; even oldies like IE5 and Netscape Communicator 4 seem hard to eradicate).

As if that isn't enough, each browser has settings and plugins that make them behave differently in different situations, and behavior can even change between the same version of a browser, on different operating systems.

The server environment is usually within our control, or at least we know what that environment will be. The client environment however is usually beyond our control and hard to predict. If you are developing an application that will be used by a specific set of users (e.g. an intranet application or a business application), you may have more information regarding what browsers are being used but with open applications and web sites, prepare to encounter a variety of browsers.

When testing the application, test it on a variety of browsers. In particular when you use techniques that have a higher chance of browser incompatibility, such as JavaScript or some less common CSS constructs, make sure to test on all browser environments that you expect to encounter.

Virtualization products such as VMWare or Xen can help test different browsers and operating systems, and make it easy to share these environments among the development team. To speed up testing, multiple browsers can be combined in a single virtual machine. This way, you can have a Windows virtual machine running Firefox 2, IE7 and Opera 9, one running Firefox 1, IE6, Opera 8, etc. It takes some time to set up a good set of virtual machines, but when ready, it's a matter of adding a virtual machine when new browser versions are released. During the early phases of a development project, you should make a list of browsers that you need to support, and when testing, you can boot up the relevant virtual machines and test.

In a team with multiple testers, you can reduce the amount of time that cross-browser testing takes by having the testers each use a different browser. It is also a good idea to have the developers use different browsers during development.

Other useful tools that can help with browser testing:

- There is a plugin for Firefox called *ietab* that can switch rendering engines between IE and Firefox, without leaving Firefox: `https://addons.mozilla.org/en-US/firefox/addon/1419`.

- There are sites that can render a web site in many different browsers, and show the results as screenshots. While this only helps with verifying the layout, and not functionality, it can be useful. A free example is: `http://browsershots.org`

To avoid browser compatibility problems during development, use the following guidelines:

- When it comes to CSS and HTML, stick to standards as much as possible.

- If you need exotic constructs, search for browser compatibility information. Many sites provide information on what works in which browser, or what to do to keep things compatible.

- When developing JavaScript, consider using an abstraction layer in the form of libraries such as Prototype (`http://www.prototypejs.org`), that already have solved the browser differences.

If you follow these simple rules, the risk of encountering browser incompatibility is reduced significantly. Nevertheless, it can never be prevented completely, so testing is essential.

Performance Testing

Chapter 6 contained some general guidelines on developing with performance in mind, and in the next chapter we will dive into optimizing the performance of a web site. In Chapter 13 we will have a look at high performance and scalable infrastructures. There's a lot of information on performance, but no matter what you do to guarantee or optimize performance, you need to test the performance of an application before you release it to a customer or the general public. Nothing is more frustrating than seeing the initial excitement of a new launch turn into a disillusion when it can't handle the load. There are three distinct types of performance that can be tested.

Responsiveness

The responsiveness of an application is measured in the amount of time it takes for a page to load. If the user needs to wait 2 seconds for a page to load, he will find the application 'sluggish'. The general principle is that the faster the page loads, the better. What is acceptable for a user however depends on the type of application or site. If the user needs to navigate around a lot, he will find wait times of a second annoying, but if it's just an article he's reading, waiting a second before it is fully loaded is more acceptable.

Often the specifications will contain requirements on the load time, which makes it easier to test: you can measure the load time against the actual requirement. If the requirements are not specified, or only in vague terms such as 'it should be fast', it's a more subjective experience and placing yourself in the position of the user and working with your application will give you a feeling of the responsiveness.

The response-time of a PHP application depends on various factors:

- The time it takes to run the script and produce output

- The time it takes to download that output to the browser

- The amount of images, JavaScript and stylesheets that are loaded

The actual PHP code is just one element, and although it's tempting to measure just that (we still encounter 'it took 0.2 seconds to generate this page' indicators on pages or in comments sometimes), for the end user only the whole package counts. A page without images that takes 2 seconds to render will feel just as sluggish as a page that renders in 0.1 seconds but contains 3Mb of images.

Note that responsiveness also depends on the number of simultaneous users: take that into account when testing the response times.

Capacity

The capacity of an application is related to responsiveness but it looks at the performance from a different perspective. Where responsiveness looks at how long it takes for one user to view a page, the capacity determines how many users the system can handle simultaneously.

It not only depends on the number of users, but also on how many pages each user requests, how many files the web server needs to serve to each user (images, stylesheets etc.). The capacity of a system determines how many servers you need to operate the web site, so we need to figure out a way to test this. A common way to measure the capacity is to determine the average number of requests per second a server can handle. If we know how many requests users will submit on average, and how many requests a server can handle, we can calculate the number of servers we need for a given number of visitors. The number of requests can easily be determined by running scripts that try to fire as many requests as they can at a server. We'll look at a few examples of useful tools later on in this chapter.

One word of caution: it is tempting to work with averages, but in many cases, visitors of a web site will not be distributed evenly across the day, or even across the week: there are web sites with morning visitors, evening visitors and web sites that have their peaks in the weekend. If you use the average in performance tests, there's a big chance the application cannot cope with the peak traffic. When calculating the numbers, try to get an average number of requests per second during "regular peaks" and compare those with the average number of requests a server can handle.

Besides the regular peaks there are always unexpected peaks; your web site may be mentioned on popular web sites such as digg.com, appear in a television program etc. Your standard infrastructure should be able to handle at least the regular peaks. If you create an architecture that should cope with a one-off fifteen minutes of fame, you'll end up with an expensive infrastructure that is idle 99.9% of the time.

It's important to have a scalable architecture so you can easily grow if you have a sudden need for more capacity. We'll dive into that in Chapter 13 (*Deployment*).

Usability

A third performance indicator we can test is the usability of the application. This is a performance element that is often forgotten, even though it is very important to end users. When we looked at responsiveness we looked at how much time it took to render a page. In the case of usability, we look at how long it takes a user to complete a task. In the case of a web-shop, an example would be the amount of time it takes to add a new product to the site. This depends on the following factors:

- The amount of actions (or clicks) a user needs to do to perform the task

- The amount of information on the screen

- The amount of forms to complete

- The amount of screens involved

- The responsiveness of each of the screens

- The importance of the time it takes to complete tasks depends on the frequency; if a product is added to a web site once a year then it is acceptable if it takes a while, but if publishing articles is your core business then you will want to be able to do it as fast as possible.

Testing the usability of an application is difficult since it is hard to automate. It's best to have a set of testers each perform tasks and measure the amount of time it takes them to complete the task. Since the task may require subject knowledge, you may also want to have the customer participate in such tests.

Stress Tests

Performance testing, especially responsiveness and capacity, can be done using automated tools. The Apache foundation has two open source tools that can be used to perform testing. The first of these tools is ab, or *Apache Bench*. This is a command line utility that takes a URL and some other parameters, performs a test by requesting the given URL a number of times (with a specified concurrency) and reports the result in, among others, the number of requests per second.

While this is a useful tool, it doesn't test real-life scenarios; it just requests the same page over and over again as fast as it can; it is useful however to see how your system performs under stress and what concurrency it can handle. It's also useful to measure the impact of changes in the application, as in the following example. Create two files, `include.php` and `otherfile.php` with the following contents:

```php
<?php
  // include.php
  include_once('otherfile.php');
?>

<?php
  // otherfile.php
  echo 'hello world';
?>
```

Run the Apache Bench command (if you have Apache installed, `ab` can usually be found in its bin directory):

```
ab -c 50 -n 1000 http://yourserver/include.php
```

This will request the file 1000 times, with a concurrency of 50 (it will simulate 50 users requesting the file exactly at the same time).

Now change the `include.php` code to this:

```php
<?php
  // include.php
  include('otherfile.php');
?>
```

Rerun the same `ab` command, and notice the difference in number of requests per second. (This is caused by the file system operations that include_once needs to perform, but that's a subject for a different chapter). This demonstrates one of the possible uses of Apache Bench as an automated performance test tool. More Apache Bench information can be found at `http://httpd.apache.org/docs/2.0/programs/ab.html`.

The Zend Platform discussed in other parts of this book contains a web-based front-end to Apache Bench that makes it easy to run benchmarks without having to remember the `ab` parameters.

For more real-life tests, have a look at Apache Flood. Like Apache Bench, this is a free open source tool for benchmarking web sites, but the major difference is that Apache Flood is "profile driven". In the real world, your web sites or applications will be visited by different visitors. Some may order products, others may search the product catalog, and the rest is just reading the content on the site. In Apache Flood, you store such scenarios in a configuration file in the form of user profiles. Then you can run a test based on these profiles, so actual users are simulated. This gives more realistic results than Apache Bench. Apache Flood can be found at `http://httpd.apache.org/test/flood/`

There are many more tools that can help with performance testing. There are some compelling commercial solutions that have similar features to Apache Flood, combined with a professional GUI to configure test suites. Some of these work with 'populations'. You can create user profiles and run an automated test using groups of users from a certain profile. For example, you might want to run an extensive performance test with 1000 regular visitors, 20 people placing an order and 100 people searching a product catalog, and see the impact of such a scenario on the system. A list of such tools can be found at Wikipedia (`http://en.wikipedia.org/wiki/Web_server_benchmarking`). Most of them are not PHP specific, and can test any web application.

One final word on performance testing: test with a significant data set; your database will start relatively empty and in that case, most queries will be lightning fast anyway. Make some predictions on the size of your data and test with at least that amount. This way, you not only test with relevant visitor numbers, but also with relevant amounts of data.

Automated Testing

One of the major problems with testing is the amount of time it takes. So far in this chapter we have seen many ways to test an application and many areas that we need to cover when testing. While this has a very positive impact on the quality of the system, it can be a very time consuming operation.

If we make a small change to the application, this may have a significant impact on the rest of the system so it's usually not sufficient to just test that change; you should repeat the tests for the rest of the system. The larger the project, the bigger this problem becomes; to an extent where a change that took two hours to develop requires six hours to retest the functionality that was impacted by the change.

The main cause for this testing overhead is that testing requires a lot of manual labor. To solve the problem, we will look at ways to automate the testing process. We already looked at some tools when we covered performance tests, but the other tests we discussed are far more labor intensive, so we are going to want to automate those as well. There are a number of ways to do that.

Unit Tests

A *unit test* is a script that tests a part of the code. Typically, a unit test checks if, given certain inputs, the output is in line with what we expect. Let's look at a small example. We have developed a function that we want to test:

```
/**
 * Given a a 2-letter ISO country code, it returns the full name
 * of the country.
 * @param String $isocode
 * @return String The full country name, or an empty string
 *                 if not found.
 */
function getCountryName($isocode)
{
  ....
}
```

There are a number of situations we can test. In a unit test, we combine those tests in a test-case:

```
function getCountryNameTest()
{
  assertTrue(getCountryName('NL')=='The Netherlands');
  assertTrue(getCountryName('QQ')==='');
```

```
    assertTrue(getCountryName(234)==='');
}
```

As you can see, we not only test the situation that works (when testing manually, developers are often tempted to test only this situation), but we also test if the result is what we expect when we use it in other situations. The documented behavior of the function is that it returns an empty string if it doesn't find anything, so we test that as well. It shouldn't return false or NULL; this might be equally valid, but it is not inline with expectations, so we test against it. Now, if someone changes the code of the getCountryName function, he can run this test to see if the behavior of the function remains consistent in all known scenarios.

If you try to run the above example, you will notice it doesn't work out of the box, because assertTrue is not a valid PHP function. There is an `assert` function in PHP that you can use to evaluate results, or you can develop your own `assertTrue` function, but it's easier to use a Unit Test framework which provides this functionality for you. A Unit Test framework provides assertions for all known results: assert if something is true or false, assert if a variable has a certain type, assert if a string is equal to another string, assert if an exception was thrown, etc. Furthermore, it can run an entire suite of tests and report the results in various output formats (HTML if you run the tests from a browser, plain text if you run them on the command-line, or even XML if you need to interpret the results with some tool).

There are two major Unit Test frameworks for PHP:

- PHPUnit (`http://www.phpunit.de`). This is the most popular unit test framework for PHP. It was written by Sebastian Bergmann, one of the leading unit test experts from the PHP community. PHPUnit is integrated in several IDEs, and one of its main advantages over the other frameworks is that it has support for test-metrics; for example, it can indicate what percentage of the code your test-cases are covering.

- SimpleTest (`http://simpletest.sourceforge.net/`). SimpleTest is very similar to PHPUnit, but doesn't have metrics support. But on the other hand, SimpleTest has "web test" support, which PHPUnit doesn't. We'll have a closer look at web tests in the next section.

Whichever you use is a matter of taste to some extent. The way they work is very similar, and with a little effort test-cases written for one can be converted to test-cases for the other. If you like metrics, PHPUnit is the better choice at the moment, but usually it is just a matter of time before the other framework catches up and offers similar functionality. PHPUnit has the advantage that the integration with other tools such as IDEs is currently stronger.

Web Tests

Unit tests are low level. They test the functions and methods of an application. If every function and method in a system is properly tested, then the chances of bugs at a higher level are minimized, but not eliminated. Higher level tests, such as functional tests by users of the system, can be automated too.

A *web test* is a test-case that simulates a visitor or user and clicks through the application. Like unit tests, web tests can make assertions to evaluate if the test passed or failed. In a web test, possible assertions to make include:

- Does the page contain certain key elements? For instance, does it contain valid a valid HTML document? Does a form contain a submit button, or is specific content present?

- Is the application flow correct? For example, are we seeing a "thank you" page after we submitted a contact form, or are we getting a customer detail screen when we perform a check-out in a web-shop?

- Are the headers correct? Are we getting the proper caching/non-caching headers for static/dynamic pages? Is the code sending a proper redirect header?

We can hook test-cases into the functions of the application that output data, but testing at the user level is often more practical, in particular if the application uses things like CSS and JavaScript to create the user interface.

One such powerful web test suite is Selenium (`http://selenium.openqa.org/`). Selenium is a set of tools that can record a test-case and replay them automatically. Using the recorder you click through the application and record the scenario that you want to test. Then, you run the recorded test-case periodically to check if the application remains operational. Selenium can run test-cases on a variety of web-browsers and operating systems, so you can do automated environment testing as well.

Note that Selenium tests the functionality of an application in different browsers, but does not check if the layout is consistent across browsers. Layout consistency checks are currently hard to automate.

Test-Driven Development

The classic problem with testing is that usually it's done at the very end of a project. If we have a setback and things take longer than we expect, but our deadline is close and we can't or won't shift the deadline, then testing is usually the item that gets cut. We ship a half tested, or even untested, product, because we don't want to disappoint the customer by blowing the deadline. Often this backfires. The quality is not what the customer expects, things break, especially since we rushed in some last-minute features and we didn't have time to test their impact on the rest of the system, and the customer starts wondering if we have tested the product at all before we shipped it to him.

It takes some courage and a convincing story if we want to tell the customer that we want to extend the deadline because we want to work on the quality of the product, and it helps if we do this in good time rather than one day before the supposed deadline. However, many customers will respect your decision because it's in their best interest, and the disappointment they will have is probably less than their disappointment would have been, had they received your half-tested end result.

If this scenario sounds familiar, you may want to have a look at *test-driven development*. This is a development methodology that puts testing at the heart of development. Instead of testing at the end of the development life-cycle, testing is an integral part of the development.

The Process

Test-driven development roughly means taking the following steps:

- First, you create a test-case that tests the software you are going to write.

- Then, you run all test-cases you have so far, and you will notice that all of them pass, except the newly created test-case. (if it doesn't, your test-case is wrong; you haven't developed the new code yet so it should fail.)

- Next, you write the code so it satisfies your test.

- You run your test-cases again, and this time, the new test-case will pass.

- If it doesn't pass at first, refactor the code until it does.

The Result

This approach ensures that you are testing while you write the code. It also ensures that the quality of the software remains high, as you continuously re-run all test-cases. Any negative impact of new code on the existing system will result in failing test-cases. The most important benefit from this approach is that testing is not something you skip at the end when the deadline is near; it is so interwoven into the development process, that the software is continuously tested.

Another benefit is that the software will be more modular and better testable. In general, this helps improve the design of the code. When done properly, you don't write any code that you don't need. There's no "just in case" code, because you just write the code to satisfy your test-cases. If your test-cases are solid, and test everything the software should do, then just passing the test-cases is sufficient. This helps prevent code bloat.

I've only scratched the surface of Test-Driven Development (TDD). There are 2 books I recommend on this subject:

- "Test Driven Development: By Example" by Kent Beck (`http://www.mypearsonstore.com/bookstore/product.asp?isbn=0321146530`). Kent Beck is the creator of the popular "Extreme Programming" methodology (we'll look at that later in this book). TDD is an integral part of Agile methodologies such as XP. In the book, Kent uses Java and Python examples. That is not PHP, but Python is a scripting language too and the examples can as such easily be applied to PHP.

- "PHP in Action" by Dagfinn Reiersøl, Marcus Baker and Chris Shiflett (`http://www.manning.com/reiersol/`). This book, which covers many PHP related subjects, has a part on TDD and its use in PHP. Marcus Baker, author of the SimpleTest framework, is one of the authors of this book.

Continuous Integration

After you've been doing unit testing for a while, you'll want to take automated testing one step further. Instead of every developer running the test-cases when they have developed something, you can automate the test execution. Continuous integration means that software is continuously integrated and tested. If someone commits a change, the unit-tests are automatically executed and feedback is provided. The idea was developed by the people behind Test Driven Development and the Extreme Programming methodology. The principles of Continuous Integration are:

- The product becomes more stable because unit-tests are executed with each change in the code base.

- The developer has early feedback from the changes he commits.

For a developer, one of the benefits from continuous integration is that he doesn't have to run an entire test suite for each change that he wants to commit; this is done automatically by the build system. In many programming languages continuous integration means that you need an automated build procedure that compiles and builds the software every time, but for PHP, it's much simpler. "Building" a PHP application is a matter of checking it out from the source code repository.

So in order to perform Continuous Integration in PHP, you need to be using source control software and you need to have a significant amount of unit tests for your application.

Firstly, make sure the test suite can run from the command line, and hook up the execution of the tests to an SVN hook so that on each commit, a test-run is started. Based on the result of the test, you can take action, for example send a test-report to developers that did a faulty commit (or even automatically block the commit), or just report statistics on the build quality.

Instead of building your own Continuous Integration environment, you could use an existing set of tools to build one. The most commonly used tools are:

- CruiseControl (`http://cruisecontrol.sourceforge.net/`). CruiseControl is a generic continuous integration tool that works for almost any technology. With the phpUnderControl add-on (`http://www.phpundercontrol.org/`), CruiseControl is adapted specifically for a PHP environment, and provides test-metrics that are useful for PHP developers. phpUnderControl requires you to use PHPUnit for the unit tests.

- Xinc (`http://code.google.com/p/xinc/`). Xinc is short for "Xinc is not CruiseControl". It is a Continuous Integration system similar to CruiseControl, but written specifically for PHP. It's also written entirely in PHP, so it's easier to customize for PHP developers.

Writing a Test Plan

In this chapter we have covered many things we should test, and many ways to do so. Which ones you are going to use depends on your project. As a final recommendation in this chapter on Quality Assurance I would like to recommend writing a test plan. This doesn't have to be a fancy 100 page document (on the contrary, the shorter the better), but it's useful to document your test procedures.

- First, because the entire team will be able to see how they are expected to do quality control on the product. New developers can easily get accustomed to the test procedures that are in place, by reading the document and the reasoning behind the procedures.

- Second, it is useful for the customer. If the customer knows that quality is a key issue of the project, and that the quality of his product is guarded with a number of procedures, this will add to his confidence.

In general, the following things should be documented in a test plan:

- Scope: What is, and what isn't tested.

- Method: How the tests are performed.

- Responsibility: Who will perform the tests and who will take action if tests fail.

- Reporting: How test results are communicated to the customer or the team.

If you write this down, you will find that testing will be less ad hoc and the quality of the software will improve.

Chapter 12

Optimization

When an application is finished, and the number of users or visitors starts to increase, you may find yourself in the need for optimizing the application. In previous chapters we have already seen how we can take performance into account during development, but still there might be situations that require optimization at a later stage. If you've performed the performance tests described in Chapter 11, and the result was not in line with the requirements, you may have to optimize. There are various ways to optimize applications, and this chapter describes some of them.

Profiling

Before we start optimizing an application, we first have to know where the bottlenecks are. A good way to do this is using a profiler. There are two major profilers available for PHP :

- Xdebug has a built-in profiler (http://xdebug.org/docs/profiler)

- Zend Studio has a built-in profiler (http://www.zend.com/en/products/studio/)

Both profilers work in a similar way. They run a PHP script and collect timing information. The following metrics are collected by the profiler:

- How long each function call takes. It measures both the time spent in the code from the function itself ('own' or 'self' time) and the total time that was spent in calls to other functions or includes of other PHP files.

- How often each function is called.

- How much time is spent in certain functions relative to the rest of the script.

It is important to look at both the time and the number of calls; a function that takes 0.1 second but that is called a 1000 times, is worse than a function that takes 0.5 seconds which is called only once. Both profilers take the number of times a function is called and the time it takes and combine this in a metric indicating the number of total seconds spent in the function.

The relative metrics are useful because they tell you that for example, 10% of the total script execution time is caused by a specific function.

The following screenshot is sample output of the Zend Studio profiler, when I run it on one of my applications. This depicts the 'graph' view, which gives a quick overview of how the performance of an application is distributed over the PHP files.

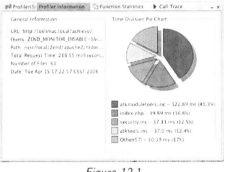

Figure 12.1

A graphical file view isn't always useful, as files can be big and still not point you to the bottlenecks, but it gives a nice first indication of where our performance bottlenecks are located. The following screenshot is what you get when you zoom in to the function level:

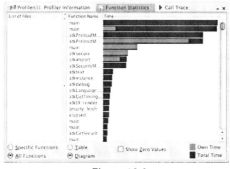

Figure 12.2

By sorting the call list based on time spent, with the slowest on top, we immediately have an overview of the bottlenecks of the application. Spending time on these areas will have impact and is worth investigating.

A profiler helps us focus on the bottlenecks. Often, performance optimizations are done on functions that we think are slow, but in the grand scheme of things, appear to be negligible. Likewise, a function that we think is fast can still cause problems if it is called thousands of times in a loop. Both are examples of issues that a profiler can help us find.

Developers that are looking for performance problems without a profiler often add timing information in the code, by calling some log function that records the time. The disadvantage of such a "manual" profiler is that we add code to measure the performance, meaning that we first make it worse (technically, the profiler also has a slight performance overhead; but this is only small). Another disadvantage is that we cannot easily do this on a live environment.

Caching

By far the most successful way to optimize an application is caching. It can be used to reduce system load, reduce page load times, and in general is a good way to avoid doing things multiple times during a request, and even to avoid doing things on every request. There are several forms of caching, which we'll look at in this chapter.

Opcode Caching

Opcode caching, or "acceleration" as it is often called, can best be explained by describing the problem that it solves.

Let's take a look at what happens when a user requests a webpage that is generated by a PHP script. The technical details are a bit more complicated, but roughly, the following happens:

- The user's browser sends a request to the web server, and tells it that it wants to have the contents from a certain URL, say, `http://yoursite.com/index.php`.

- The web server detects it's a PHP file, and passes the request to the PHP interpreter.

- PHP reads the index.php file from disk.

- PHP compiles the file into a binary (executable) representation (so-called 'opcodes').

- PHP runs the code.

In step 5, the code that the developers have written is actually executed. Step 3 and 4 are needed to be able to do step 5. PHP code is readable by programmers, but it needs to be compiled into a form that the server can execute. Many languages such as C work with a compiler: the programmers compile the code before it is released. PHP however is an *interpreted language*, meaning that you don't have to compile the code beforehand; this is done by PHP whenever it's needed. The obvious advantage of this is that you can easily make changes to a PHP application. Just make the change, and you're ready to go. The disadvantage is that there's some overhead incurred when compiling the code on the fly. How much overhead depends on the complexity and size of the code.

Once an application is in production stage, the code doesn't change that often, but still for every page request steps 3 and 4 are done, over and over again. This is where opcode caching can be used. An opcode cache basically stores the result of step 3 and 4 in an intermediary file (or in memory). It stores the compiled code so PHP can directly execute the code, without having to compile it every time. It does keep track of changes in the code. If the code changes, the file is automatically recompiled.

What's nice about this is that it combines the benefit of an interpreted language (developers can just change the code and do not need to recompile), with the benefit of a compiled language (compilation of the code, which can be relatively time consuming, is not done on each request). The impact of opcode caching depends heavily on the application. But in many cases, compiling the PHP code is more complex than actually executing it, so it's not uncommon to have a performance increase of a factor 2, by just using opcode caching.

To make use of opcode caching you need to install an *accelerator*. There are several accelerators available, with subtle differences in the way they work, but in general they all follow the same principle. For developers, this is usually completely transparent. They do not need to change anything in their code, and the application behaves the same whether it's running with or without an accelerator. It's just faster.

Below is a list of the major accelerators:

- APC (`http://www.php.net/manual/en/ref.apc.php`)

- eAccelerator (`http://eaccelerator.net/`)

- ionCube PHP Accelerator (`http://www.php-accelerator.co.uk/`)

- xCache (`http://trac.lighttpd.net/xcache/`)

- Zend Accelerator (available as part of Zend Platform) (`http://www.zend.com/en/products/platform/`)

Output Caching

In the previous section, we've seen a way to skip the "read the PHP file and compile it" part of PHP execution. The main reason we can skip this part is that the code doesn't change that often. We can take that a step further. In many applications, the output of the PHP scripts doesn't change that often either. Consider a common Content Management scenario. There's a back-end where editors edit their web site, and there's the front-end that the visitors see. The data is stored in a database by the back-end, and the front-end retrieves it and displays it.

It is quite likely that the data in the database doesn't change that often. Maybe it changes once a day, or even once a week. Your site has many visitors per day, so the front-end code would be pulling the same data from the database, and rendering the same page over and over again, hundreds, thousands, or even millions of times a day. To stop wasting resources on things that don't change, you can use *output caching*. Output caching is easy. There are products available that can help, but often a solution as easy as storing the output of a script as a static HTML file will suffice. An easy way to store the output of a script is to capture it using PHP's *output buffering* mechanism:

```php
<?php

  if (file_exists('cache/page.html'))
  {
    $output = file_get_contents('cache/page.html');
  }
  else
  {
    ob_start();

    // normal application logic goes here

    $output = ob_get_clean();
    file_put_contents('cache/page.html', $output);
  }

  echo $output;

?>
```

This very basic example demonstrates how an application can essentially be wrapped inside a few lines of code that take care of the output caching. The `ob_start`/`ob_get_clean` methods capture any content that is output between them, and `file_put_contents`/`file_get_contents` are used to store the result in a cache-file or to retrieve it. (Alternatives are possible where instead of `file_get_contents` you call `include()`, which saves the overhead of first writing it to a variable.)

Naturally, you will want to refactor such code into a slightly more generic version that you can easily reuse throughout an application. Often that is not necessary: many PHP libraries and frameworks have caching solutions already built in. What's important to realize is that output caching is almost always useful. Often I have had discussions with developers who say: "This is the news section. News is very dynamic." It isn't. The views-to-edit ratio for news sites, especially the really popular ones, is still enormous. When content does change, you can clear the cache on the fly.

There is a lot of information on content caching to be found using Google. The following article by Alejandro Gervasio is a nice how-to that explains the concept of content caching by using PHP's built in 'output buffering' mechanism. The article is from 2005 but is still relevant and can be found at `http://www.devshed.com/c/a/PHP/Output-Caching-with-PHP`.

More information on PHP's output buffering mechanism can be found here at `http://www.php.net/manual/en/ref.outcontrol.php`.

Note that in high-performance web sites, even reading from/writing to a file can be considered costly. For a high-performance setup you might want to store the cache in memory instead of in files. In the next section, we will examine a few products that can help with caching in memory.

Data Caching

As easy as caching the entire output of a script may seem in the previous section, in reality, things might be more complicated. In this book we're talking about enterprise development, so we will go beyond the common basic CMS scenario. Consider a customer portal that takes its data from various sources. A database from the Content Management System, a web service from the CRM system, an XML interchange with a financial application and a whole arsenal of other systems that contain information on a customer.

In this case, it's no longer easy to say "the data changes every day so let's cache for a day." The CRM system might change once a week whereas the financial application might change whenever a bank transaction occurs, and we would want our customers to see accurate order status on the portal. Still, the financial application may be slow, and connecting to it to retrieve payment status information might take two seconds. Contacting the CRM system takes another second and when combined, rendering a page in the portal might take five seconds to display. An application that takes five seconds to render a page will be considered sluggish, so we have to find a solution.

We might say: "let's cache indefinitely, and refresh the cache whenever something actually changes," so the user almost always sees a pre-generated version that is accurate to the last change. This approach would require the external applications to trigger the cache refresh and this is not always possible. The financial system may very well have a one-way connection that is only initiated from the web site (pull-mechanism), so it has no way of telling the web site to refresh its cache.

When dealing with these types of scenarios, it's better to apply *data caching* instead of full page content caching. Data caching is a way to cache only parts of the code. If you have a heavy query on a database, or a slow web service call to an external system, consider wrapping it inside a small piece of code that caches the result. This is similar to the content caching we have seen earlier, but in this case, we're only caching the output of a query, or the result of a web service call, or the return value of some function that takes a while to complete.

This approach makes it easy to have several layers of caching, that each have their own properties. Maybe the cache for the CMS content caches for a week, whereas the call to the financial system only caches for five minutes. With this more fine-grained way of caching, writing the output to a file becomes less efficient. In this case, it's better to cache in memory. Due to the stateless nature of PHP however, memory is not shared between requests. So if you store something in memory, it will vanish when the script terminates.

To solve that, you can consider some of the many memory based caching solutions. These come roughly in two flavors: distributed and local. A distributed cache is one where the data is stored on one or more dedicated servers. In other words, the PHP scripts run on servers A through E, and the cache is located on server F. The opposite, a local cache, is one where the cache is stored on the same machine as the PHP scripts that use it. In environments where only one server is used to run an application, the result is equal, but for clustered environments there is a significant difference. With local caching, if an application runs on five servers and visitors are randomly distributed over these five servers, then all five servers need a copy of the data in their cache. So even if the data is cached, we still need to calculate the result five times. An additional disadvantage is that content can become out of sync between machines, if on one machine a cache expires but not on another machine. A distributed cache on the other hand has network overhead, because for every request the servers need to fetch data from the cache server. Which of the two is more efficient heavily depends on the amount of time it takes to generate the data if it isn't cached, and the frequency of change. In large applications, often a combination of distributed and local caching is used, depending on the characteristics of the cached data. Below is a list of products that can cache data in memory.

Distributed:

- Memcached (`http://www.danga.com/memcached/` - server part, `http://www.php.net/memcache` php extension to use memcached in PHP)

Local:

- APC (`http://www.php.net/manual/en/ref.apc.php`)

- Zend Platform's Partial Page Caching (`http://www.zend.com/en/products/platform/`)

Note that APC was also listed among the opcode caching products; while intended as an opcode cache, its `apc_store/apc_fetch` functions make APC suitable for data caching as well. Also note that Memcached can also be used as a local cache if you install it on every machine; this does incur some overhead and is therefor not recommended.

One final remark on data caching: it might be tempting to use sessions to cache data between requests. It saves the hassle of having to install and configure a memory based caching solution, and it's very easy to use. I advise strongly against this. PHP's session mechanism is useful for transferring data between requests, but it is not suitable for caching; this is partly due to the way sessions are stored and partly because of the way sessions work in PHP. In any case, don't be tempted to store data in the session just because you want to cache it. It will reduce the scalability of your application in the long run, and reading a large amount of data from the session handler has a significant performance impact. Finally, sessions are per-user, which is another reason not to use the session for caching.

Read- Versus Write-based Caching

The output caching mechanism discussed above is based on the fact that the first user that needs data, will retrieve it and store it in the cache. The second user thus no longer needs to retrieve the data but can fetch it directly from the cache. Since the cache is created upon the first read, I call this *read-based caching*.

While this works well in most situations, there is a limit to the scalability of this approach. Figure 12.3 shows a read-based caching scenario.

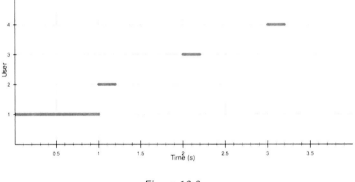

Figure 12.3

At t=0 the first user enters. There is no data in the cache yet, so his request will retrieve the data, for example from a database, and writes the cache. In this example, this takes one second. At t=1 the second user visits the same page. The content is cached, so the request takes only 0.2 seconds to complete. As you can see, the caching is very effective. There are periods between requests in which this hypothetical system does not have anything to do. Now suppose the frequency with which this particular page is retrieved doubles. Now the graph looks like that in Figure 12.4.

At t=0, the first user visits the page and starts rendering the cache. At t=0.5 however, the second user already appears. This time, the cache isn't ready yet, and the script will decide to generate it on the fly. At t=1, the third user comes along but now the cache has already been written. This is less efficient, as multiple requests are now not taken from the cache. If the frequency increases to one user every 0.3 seconds, we get what is shown in Figure 12.5.

The first 4 users all will fail to get something from the cache, and not until the fifth user comes along, we benefit from caching. Also, have a look at the concurrency of this scenario. In the first figure only one request was being serviced at any given time.

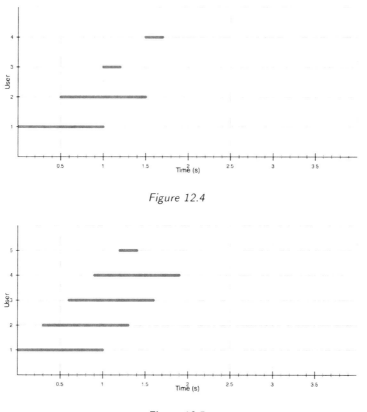

Figure 12.4

Figure 12.5

This means that a single Apache child is sufficient to serve all 4 users. In the second scenario, there are a maximum of 2 simultaneous requests at any one moment. This means that we need 2 apache children to serve 4 users. In the last scenario, there is a moment around t=0.9 where there are 4 concurrent requests. So for the first 4 users, we need 4 apache children, and caching benefits only appear after t=1.2.

This may or may not be a problem, depending on several factors. However in a high traffic environment this can become very problematic, as the system will have a difficult time handling the load when a page is removed from the cache. At that moment, many requests will simultaneously be working on an uncached version and a peak in server load will occur.

Another potential problem is locking; if the cache is written to a file, there are multiple processes working on this file. Depending on how long it takes between opening and closing the cache file, other requests may be locked and take even longer before they complete. To prevent such scenarios, you can move over to write-based caching. This means that the cache is not generated by the first user that requests a file, but whenever something in the back-end has changed. This can be a separate environment that places the cache-file on the disk, so all requests can directly use the cached version and none of them need to generate the cache.

Caching Strategies

All decisions regarding caching (read- versus write based caching, what to cache, what not to cache, cache life-time etc.) together form the *caching strategy* of a web site. The caching strategy revolves around three basic questions:

- What to cache (data, content, queries, calculations etc.)

- When to cache (upon read, upon write)

- Where to cache (disk or memory; distributed or local)

Although I've only mentioned caching in the Optimization chapter of this book, it is wise to take the caching strategy into account during the technical design phase, in particular if you know upfront that the web site is going to be high-traffic.

When defining a caching strategy, take the following things into account:

- How many requests per second do you expect to get per cached item.

- How long does it take to render an item if it's not cached.

- How long does it take to render an item if it's cached.

- How often does the item change?

- What is the read versus write ratio?

- How many variations of an item will the cache contain? (language specific versions, user specific versions etc.)

- Are there limitations to the amount of storage (memory and disk) you can use for caching?

Answering these questions for the relevant items of a web site or application will help you to define a proper caching strategy.

Background Processing

Caching speeds up things that need to be done, but don't need to be done on each request. There are also things that do not need to be done during a request at all. I'll explain with an example.

Suppose you have written a Content Management System. When a webmaster deletes a page from the CMS, a number of things may need to happen: the images on the page need to be deleted, the cache of the page needs to be refreshed or cleared, as well as the cache of pages referencing this page, the menu needs to be recompiled, etc. The most common way to program this is, in pseudo-code:

```
deletePage($pageId);
deleteImages($pageId);
clearCache($pageId);
cleanupReferences($pageId);
rebuildMenu();

echo 'The page has been deleted.';
```

In other words, everything is done sequentially and the user has to wait on all the items to complete. Many of these steps however are "maintenance" steps that the user does not necessarily have to wait for.

One solution is to perform such maintenance in the background. PHP does not feature multithreading, but there are many other ways to perform something in the background. One solution is to have a cronjob running periodically that runs background tasks. Using this technique, the code could become:

```
deletePage($pageId);
schedulePageCleanup($pageId);
echo 'The page has been deleted.';
```

This will schedule the maintenance and immediately provide feedback to the user. It requires some coding to create a scheduling system, but offloading things to the background may reduce page load times and will make the application feel faster for the users.

Unlike caching, you are not skipping anything; exactly the same amount of processing is required. The major difference is that the user no longer has to wait for it to finish. An additional advantage is that it becomes easy to offload tasks to dedicated hardware, so the web servers can concentrate on serving the webpages. Here are a few real-world scenarios where background processing is useful:

- Order processing (e.g. sending an order to the accounting software)

- Mailings (e.g. sending a message in bulk to a large number of people)

- Conversion of data (e.g. creating a flash preview of a movie, or generating different image sizes from an uploaded picture)

In addition to `cron` as a useful tool to enable background processing, there is also commercial software available that performs a similar task. For example, the enterprise edition of the Zend Platform that has been discussed earlier in this book has a feature called "Job Queues," that is built exactly for this purpose. The advantage over cron is that tasks can be dynamically scheduled using a PHP API. Cron runs periodically whereas Job Queue jobs only run when scheduled. The "Job Queue" features dependencies between jobs, which can be used for example to perform a bulk email job only if all addresses have been successfully imported beforehand.

Micro Optimization

Consider the following code snippets:

```
echo "hello world";
echo 'hello world';
```

```
for ($i = 0; $i < count($array); $i++)
for ($i = 0, $cnt = count($array); $i < $cnt; ++$i)
```

In both snippets, each of the two lines are functionally identical. They have the exact same effect in an application. However, the second variant is faster. In the first case, the echo with single quotes is faster because in a double quoted string, variables may need to be parsed, so PHP will parse these strings, whereas single quoted strings are used literally.

In the second snippet, the loop is executed depending on the number of elements in $array. In the first line, the count is done on every iteration, in the second line, this is done once before the loop. Also, ++$i is slightly faster than $i++, due to the way this is handled internally. This type of optimization is called *micro-optimization*. The difference per statement is small (usually a matter of milliseconds). How useful this is, depends on the situation. In a high-performance environment, where every millisecond counts, this type of optimization is very useful. In a server farm of 1000 servers, even an optimization of 1 percent will save 10 servers. If the code is called many times in a loop and is a significant portion of the total page rendering time, it is very useful.

In many occasions however, if no other optimizations have been done, it's probably more useful to look at database optimization (see next chapter) and caching first. On the other hand, if developers take these micro optimizations into account while writing the code, there's a slight performance advantage at virtually no cost.

Database Optimization

In dynamic web applications, the database plays an important factor in the performance of the application. Let's look at a few ways to optimize an application at the database level.

Zero Query Policy

Queries cause a significant overhead. In high-traffic environments, where every microsecond counts, queries can be taboo. This naturally depends on the application, but there are many applications or web sites that may benefit from a "Zero Query

Policy." Such a policy may define, for example, that there may be no queries on the landing pages (the pages used by most visitors to enter the site). If data needs to be retrieved to display this page, it should be cached. You can define how strict the Zero Query Policy is and where it should be applied within an application. Because of the impact queries have, you may require that any query added to the landing pages must be approved by the architect of the application.

Finding Slow Queries

To optimize slow queries, you first have to know which queries are slow. There are a number of ways to do that:

- If you are using MySQL, you can look at the MySQL "Slow Query Log". If the mysql server was started with the `log-slow-queries` option, it will generate a log file of queries that are not performing well. More information on this MySQL feature can be found at `http://dev.mysql.com/doc/refman/5.1/en/slow-query-log.html`

- In Oracle, you can use the "Automatic Database Diagnostics Monitor" (`http://www.oracle.com/technology/obe/10gr2_db_single/manage/addm/addm_otn.htm`) to find out which queries are slow. Other database vendors have similar techniques. Consult the documentation for your database or do an online search for "<your database> find slow queries".

Independent of the database, you can use the profiler that we discussed earlier in this chapter to find slow queries. If a query is causing problems, then the profiler will point you at any one of the PHP functions for accessing the database. Looking at the parameters for that function call will then tell you what query it was executing.

The Zend Platform has a "PHP Intelligence" feature which tracks query performance problems. It will generate an event with details about what script the problem is in, which line the call to the database was made and what the SQL statement was that did not perform well. Once we know what queries are causing trouble, we can try to optimize them.

Explain Plans

There are many things that influence the performance of a query. The database has many different ways to retrieve the data you need, so it tries to determine what will be the fastest way to get the results. It can directly access the table data or it can use an index; it has various ways to join tables, to sort data, and even the order in which it performs certain actions has influence on the performance. The way the database decides to retrieve the data is called a *query execution plan.*

While the database is pretty smart, it needs our help. For example, it cannot use an index if we haven't created one (at least, most databases can't). We can also write queries differently to make them run faster. Most databases can show us when they need help by implementing what is called an "explain plan" feature. Telling the database to explain its plan will tell us how it is planning to execute a query, and this gives us important information that we can use to optimize the query. For example, the plan might tell you that the database is doing a full table scan to retrieve data. This means that it has to fetch every record in the database to see if it matches our query. This is usually an indicator that an index is missing. Have a look at the query and see if you can create an index on the columns that it is matching against. For example, suppose you are executing a query like this:

```
SELECT
  title
FROM
  news_archive
WHERE
  pub_date BETWEEN '2008-01-01' AND '2008-01-31'
```

This query retrieves the titles for all news items in January 2008. If there is no index on pub_date, it will have to read the entire news_archive table and check the pub_date of each record. This will be slow, and the explain plan will tell you that it's doing a full table scan (or not using an index; the exact message depends on the database you are using).

The explain plan has a lot more information that is useful to optimize queries. Consult the documentation for your database for the complete documentation. For MySQL this documentation can be found at `http://dev.mysql.com/doc/refman/5.0/en/using-explain.html`. For other databases, I refer you to your database documentation.

Indexes

I want to focus a little on indexes. In computer science education, indexes are probably the first thing you learn about database optimization, but still many PHP developers are only vaguely aware of database indexes.

If you need data from the database that matches some criteria, it can process all the data and pick the records that match, but the larger the database, the more data it needs to process. An index is essentially a look-up table that tells the database where to find data that matches some predefined criteria. For example, in the SQL statement of the previous paragraph, an index will tell the database where data that has a certain pub_date will be located. Scanning a small index is a lot faster than scanning an entire table.

The following situations are likely candidates for indexes:

- Foreign keys. If a field references another table (a relationship between 2 tables), then an index on the foreign key is useful, as access to the table will often be based on the value of this key. For example, when retrieving order items based on the `order_id` of the order, an index should be created on `order_id` in the `order_item` table. Note that some databases implicitly create an index when you create a foreign key; others leave that up to the developer.

- `WHERE` clause elements. If you retrieve data based on a `WHERE` clause, as in the `news_archive` example from the previous paragraph, create indexes on the elements that are commonly used in the where clause.

- Sorting or grouping. Some databases benefit from indexes when they have to group or sort on a certain field.

Note that indexes also have a slight performance overhead when inserting, deleting or updating data, because indexes need to be updated too. In most scenarios however, the benefit of having an index for read operations is well worth the tiny overhead for write operations (considering that read operations are not only more intensive than write operations, but are also much more frequent in most web-applications). Do however choose your indexes carefully; an index that is never used only adds overhead.

Denormalization

In the Architecture chapter we talked about normalization and denormalization. Here I want to discuss a few ways to denormalize a data model to increase performance.

- Partitioning. The larger a table becomes, the more it will influence the performance of queries. Partitioning a table means splitting it up into multiple tables. A common example is an archive. If you have a table containing news articles, you may want to place older articles in a separate table. This way, the more recent articles that are most frequently used, are in a smaller table, which is faster when retrieving the data. Alternatively you might like to partition tables based on some criteria. For example, if you have a large customer table with customers from 3 countries, you could place the customers for each country in separate tables. Of course, this only makes sense if the common scenario is that a query deals with only the customers in one country. So when partitioning a table, have a look at how many records the database contains, what the discriminating fields are (fields that can only have particular values, such as 'type', 'country', 'status'), and if query access is commonly based on these discriminators.

- Flattening. When a query needs data from two tables, it will have to 'join' them. A join means that the database internally creates a 'cartesian product', which means that if you join a table of 1000 records with a table of 100 records, the cartesian product the database has to deal with is 1000 x 100 = 100.000 records. The more joins, and the bigger the joins, the more memory is needed to process the query. One way to improve performance is to decrease the number of records in the tables, using partitioning, but another is flattening the tables, meaning that we create a table that already contains the elements of one table and elements of the other table. This way, we don't have to join the 2 tables because their data is already combined into a single table.

Remember that in the database design chapter I recommended to be careful with denormalization. It's often better to keep the base model normalized to guard data integrity and keep the data-model clean, and to use secondary tables that are denormalized for performance reasons. The secondary tables can be populated and kept up-to-date using triggers, or in a separate process that constantly pushes the data from the normalized primary tables to the secondary denormalized tables.

Environment Optimization

So far we have looked at ways to optimize the application itself. The final element we can optimize is the environment of the application. When optimizing the environment, we can look at several elements.

Web Server

The web server is an important part of the environment, as it handles every request and hands it off to PHP for processing. Web servers have many configuration options that influence the performance. For Apache, a good resource for tuning the performance can be found at `http://httpd.apache.org/docs/2.2/misc/perf-tuning.html`

For other web servers, there are similar tuning options; consult the documentation for your web server to find out what the possibilities are.

In general, the default settings are never optimal for an environment; they are the common "work acceptably out-of-the-box" settings that are not necessarily the fastest. Therefore it's always useful to spend some time in finding the correct settings for the web server based on your actual environment and application.

Hardware

If you need to optimize the hardware of an environment, you may want to consult a system architect, because hardware tuning is a profession on its own. There are a few basic elements though that are worth knowing about:

- The faster the CPU, the faster PHP code will run in general. However, PHP code on a single core runs just as fast as on a dual core; since PHP doesn't do multithreading, it will only use a single processor core for a single request.

On the other hand, if you have more cores, The web server will be able to run more processes simultaneously and hence the server capacity is increased. So the general rule of thumb is: the faster the better, however clich?d that may sound.

- The more memory a server has, the more simultaneous processes it can handle. Thus, more memory means more capacity. (There is a limit however to how much memory is useful; depending on the web server configuration, there's a maximum amount of memory that will be used.)

Compared to a database, PHP scripts are often more CPU intensive. If you have to choose between investing in memory and CPU power, I would choose CPU power for web servers and memory for database servers. Naturally, if your budget allows it, invest in both.

Network

In PHP applications, network traffic plays an important role. There's all kinds of traffic: there is data going from the database to the application, output going from the application to the user, input from the user to the application and if there's a central cache there may be data going from the cache over the network to the servers.

One way to optimize the network traffic is to separate the networks into several subnets. This way, data going from the database to the application doesn't interfere with the traffic from users. The traffic from the application to the user can be optimized by compressing it before it is sent. This means that the content is zipped before it is transferred to the client. The browser then unzips it when it receives the data. Since most output of PHP scripts is HTML data, which is essentially plain text, it can be compressed very efficiently. This means that the bandwidth of an application or web site can be significantly reduced, and thus, less traffic goes over the network, and sending the data to the client takes less time.

There are a number of ways to compress the output.

-Using the compression feature of the web server. Apache has a module called `mod_deflate` which can compress the output before it is sent to the browser. Some older browsers cannot cope with compression, and you can configure `mod_deflate` to skip compression for those browsers. Documentation for `mod_deflate` can be found at `http://httpd.apache.org/docs/2.2/mod/mod_deflate.html`.

- Using PHP's built-in output buffering with an `ob_gzhandler`. By buffering the output of the script, using a call to `ob_start("ob_gzhandler")`, the output will be compressed before it is sent over the network. What's nice about this feature is that this feature is smart: if the visitor has a browser that does not support compression, the output handler will not compress the output.

- Using Zend Platform's output compression feature. The difference with the other 2 solutions is that Zend Platform combines compression with its cache; if something is in the cache, it's only compressed once before it is stored in the cache, as opposed to compressing it on each requests like the other 2 solutions.

Note that compression has a slight overhead on CPU usage, because the content needs to be compressed. Carefully compare the benefits of compression (less bandwidth) to the (small) penalty on CPU usage.

Storage

Files play an important role in most applications. The files containing the PHP code, images, stylesheets, HTML, cache files, all of them are stored on a disk. Compared to memory, disks are slow. When optimizing an application, have a look at the disk configuration, and what is stored where. If you cache in files, it will be faster if you write the cache to the local disk, even if the source files of the applications are served from a network file system or an external storage. Preferably, use a memory based solution for caching.

Browser

The web-browser is as much part of the application environment as the server it is hosted on. Unfortunately, it is not an aspect that we have much influence on. "This web site is best viewed in browser X" is very nineties and not something that's really appreciated today. We have to accept the fact that people use different browsers. Luckily, we're talking about performance optimization here, and this is not really dependent on which browser people use. There are a number of standards that influence the way browsers work with our application, such as headers we can send to tell the browser how long certain elements can be cached.

By sending the proper cache headers, the browser can use its local cache. In addition to the caching we already do on the server side, this further alleviates the pressure on our application. The following headers are useful to send from a PHP application:

- `Cache-control`—this tells the browser whether or not to cache a page.

- `Last-Modified`—this tells the browser when a page was last modified. The browser can use this to check if the version in its cache needs updating.

There are also some headers that the browser sends which we can use to determine if we need to send a page back or not:

- `If-Modified-Since`—the browser will include this header if it already had a version in its cache, and will include the time-stamp of the version in the cache. We can use this value to determine if the content we have now is newer. If not, we can tell the browser not to fetch the page, and stop after the header.

It's worth investing some time in determining the proper headers for your application. By default, most PHP applications are dynamic and the browser will not cache a lot, but many pages are fairly static and change infrequently, so it might be worth having the browser cache those pages. Note that there's a major functional difference between server-side and client-side caching: at the server, you're in control of clearing the cache when you need to; on the client, you are not. If a page is cached in the browser, you are not able to tell it to remove it from its cache. Dealing with the browser cache can be tricky and confusing at times. The Mozilla web site has a nice tutorial on browser caching and headers that can be found at `http://www.mozilla.org/projects/netlib/http/http-caching-faq.html`.

Premature Optimization

Donald Knuth, author of "The Art of Computer Programming"[1], is often misquoted as saying: "Premature optimization is the root of all evil." I'll get to the real quote

---

[1] See: `http://en.wikipedia.org/wiki/The_Art_of_Computer_Programming`

in a minute, but what is meant here is that you should never optimize prematurely. Spending too much time on optimization before you run into the first performance problem can make an application less maintainable, and adds an extra level of complexity.

"First make it work, then make it fast." is a similar quote with the same underlying message. The benefit of making it work first and then optimizing it is that you will focus on the real bottlenecks. Unless you can determine exactly what your bottlenecks are going to be upfront, optimizing early on in the process will lead you to spend time on areas that wouldn't be the biggest bottlenecks. What Donald Knuth really said was: "We should forget about small efficiencies, say about 97% of the time: premature optimization is the root of all evil." This leaves room for situations where premature optimization is a viable option.

I tend to draw the line based on the requirements. If a feature requirement lists mostly the functionality without any specific performance requirement, my advice would be to make it work first, before you make it fast. On the other hand, if a requirement has a specific performance requirement, you should take this into account early on in the design phase. With specific performance requirements, your design should be such that the application can meet them. Making it work first might mean that you cannot meet the performance requirement because the performance requires a wholly different approach. This is especially the case with applications or web-sites that will be high-traffic and that contain challenging functionality that needs careful consideration in terms of caching and optimization.

One of the well-known members of the PHP community, Shahar Evron, has an interesting post on premature optimization in relation to PHP applications and can be found at `http://prematureoptimization.org/blog/archives/26`. Coincidentally, the blog itself is called Premature Optimization too.

Chapter 13

Deployment

Once an application is developed, it needs to be deployed. Deployment is the process of placing the application on the server environment. This may seem trivial, and for some applications it is; however the larger the application becomes, or the bigger the team that works on it, the more important it becomes to structure the deployment of the application. Before we can deploy an application, we need something to deploy it to: the servers.

Hosting Infrastructure

This book is about the software development life-cycle of PHP applications, so I don't want to dive too deeply into the hardware side of things, but some aspects of it will be relevant to the development life-cycle, so I will focus on these.

System Architecture

In its most simple form, a server for PHP applications is a single server that runs both the PHP application and the database. Many applications are small enough even to be able to share a server with other applications or web sites. These so-called "shared hosting" servers are more complex than single dedicated servers, since security measures need to be taken to ensure that one application doesn't meddle with another. Especially on public shared hosting servers, where the applications belong to many different parties, this can be challenging. Luckily, if you host the application on a shared server at a hosting provider, it's the responsibility of the hosting provider, and not your team, to deal with this. Don't assume though that everything is fine; check the hosting environment and contact the hosting provider about any issues.

On the other end of the spectrum, we have the big clusters of servers. Popular web sites or applications are simply too heavy to run on a single machine. System architecture here is challenging, because you have many considerations, such as distributing visitors over multiple servers randomly, synchronizing files across the cluster, and much more. We'll look at clustering a little closer in the next section.

If your team is responsible for designing the architecture of the system, make sure to involve at least the application architect, a hardware expert and a network expert, as these three aspects together form the cluster. (If you have a guru who can handle all three; that's fine, but at least make sure that you do not design an architecture if any of these roles is missing.)

Abstraction

Because the system architecture may change over time, it's a good idea to develop applications in such a way that they are independent of the underlying architecture. This way, an application can grow from a single server, to a solution with a separate database and separate web server, to a big cluster of hundreds of machines, without having to rewrite large parts of it.

To accomplish this, make sure that everything that depends on the infrastructure is abstracted into an abstraction layer. To illustrate this with an example: one of the things commonly scaled into multiple machines is the database. If you have a single database server, you just connect to that server and execute the queries. If the database is too heavy for a single machine, you can have multiple database servers in what is called a "replication" setup. Replication uses one master server that replicates its data to one or more slave servers. The slave servers are read-only, and serve the majority of the webpages, and updates and inserts are done on the master server. Without an abstraction layer, you would have to change every query in the system to either connect to the master or the slave database. If you use a database abstraction layer, you have only one class to modify, and you can implement a routine that transparently connects to the master server for update/insert queries, and to the slave server for read queries. Thus, the application itself is no longer aware of the fact that the database is setup with replication. If you work with an abstraction layer from the start, it has virtually no extra development cost; and when the application grows from one database into a cluster, the changes are small and only in a small part of the code-base. If you do a similar thing for other aspects that are depending on the infrastructure, such as file system access and sessions, your application is easily scalable when the need arises.

Clustering

In general, there are two major reasons to work with a cluster of machines; one is high availability (if one machine goes down, the other can take over), the other is performance. Because it's easier to talk about if we can work from an example, have a look at Figure 13.1, which illustrates a high availability, scalable architecture we commonly apply.

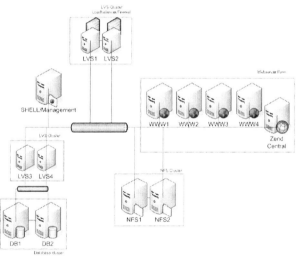

Figure 13.1

Note that this is a sample; for each situation, a different architecture is required. However this generic architecture illustrates a few common aspects in clustering.

Horizontal Scalability

The system architecture drawing depicts a *horizontally scalable* architecture. What this means is that the size of the cluster can grow linearly with an increase in visitors. If the database is overloaded, you can add a machine to the database cluster; if the web servers are overloaded, more web servers can easily be added. If more or faster storage is required, the storage can be scaled without any impact on the rest of the architecture.

The benefit of separating the architecture in layers like this is that you can more efficiently purchase hardware for a specific task. In the single-server environment, you need a server that can handle everything; in the clustered environment, each machine has a specific purpose. The database servers for example, should be heavy beasts with loads of memory. The web servers on the other hand can be fairly simple, they just need processing power. Since the web servers are the most likely to grow, this is more cost-effective.

High Availability

The architecture depicted here has a high availability. Everything that is critical to the operation of the system has redundancy; the web servers, the load balancers (the machines marked 'LVS' in Figure 13.1) and the database servers.

In this scenario, the extra machines are not only used for high availability but also for performance. There is an important thing to take into account in such a scenario: if a server goes down, make sure you not only have machines that take over, but also that the remaining servers are capable of handling the load. If the cluster constantly operates at 95% percent of its capacity, and a machine goes down, the remaining servers might not be able to handle that load. (It's OK to become a little slower of course, but going down is not an option in a high availability setup.)

If you design a cluster to be highly available, calculate a certain amount of over-capacity, directly related to the capacity of a single server. For example, if you have 2 database servers and downtime is unacceptable, then 1 server needs to be able to handle the load of the entire system in the case of failure, which means you need to have an overcapacity of 100%. If you have 11 web servers and one goes down, the remaining 10 need to be able to handle the load, so you need to have an overcapacity of only 10% (ten servers can handle the node, you need 1 extra; hence 10% overcapacity).

High availability comes with a cost. Not only is a cluster like this more difficult to maintain, you also need to have a lot more hardware. The smaller the cluster, the higher the cost of creating overcapacity. High availability should therefor be considered in relation to the cost. If being down for a day costs $20,000 in revenue loss, but it costs $120,000 to create a cluster that would've prevented this, you might want to settle for a slightly lower uptime requirement.

One final note on high availability: if a site, especially a revenue generating one, is down, the customer is not going to be happy with downtime. A likely quote: "you guarantee 99.9% uptime and we just lost $2,000 because the web site was down". I like to look at uptime percentages not only based on time, but also based on revenue loss. If a web site has a targeted turnover of ten million dollars a year, a 99.9% uptime means that you need to realize that 0.1% of that amount is "acceptable" in downtime, and should be taken into account when doing the calculations. 0.1% of ten million still is $10,000. If initially you have an uptime of 99.0%, every 0.1% that you add secures $10,000. Calculations like this help in determining how much investment a client should make in high availability.

Load Balancing

Load balancing is, as the name implies, a way to balance the load between servers. Load balancers are usually dedicated devices that take care of this. As an alternative to dedicated load balancers, you can use a small Linux server that acts as an LVS (Linux Virtual Server). LVS is open source load balancer software that can turn any Linux server into a sophisticated load balancer. You can find more information about LVS at `http://www.linuxvirtualserver.org/`.

The basic concept of load balancing is very simple; the load balancer sits in front of the servers and when a request comes in, it selects a server in the farm based on some condition (or randomly).

In the example scenario we're dealing with in this chapter, we can see three load balancers (all of which are redundant). One distributes visitors over the web farm, another distributes database requests over the database slaves and the third one distributes the use of the NFS servers. The general criteria a load balancer uses to determine which server to send a request to are:

- The status of the machines; most load balancers are smart enough not to send requests to machines that have gone down.

- The load of the machines; some load balancers can lead visitors to those machines that are the least busy.

- Round robin; in this case the load balancer sends each request to the next server in order to spread the load.

- Stickiness; Load balancers often have a feature that can keep a user on a certain machine. If one request was served by machine 42, then the subsequent requests of the same visitor will be served by server 42 as well.

Some load balancers use a combination of these.

The cheapest and easiest to configure are round robin load balancers. Sometimes however you are dealing with resources during a session that you can't transfer from one machine to the other, for example if you have written data to a local file on the machine the user is visiting. In that case, you need a sticky load balancer.

Sticky load balancers have a few disadvantages though. If a user is doing heavy operations, for example creating calculation intensive reports, he will do so on the same server. This server receives all the load from this power user, while the rest of the servers may be idle. Another disadvantage is that if a machine goes down, all requests are sent to the remaining servers. This is initially a good thing; however, because of the stickiness users will stay on the remaining servers even if the machine that went down comes back up. So this machine is now idling, while the rest is under higher load. It will take a little while before the load is distributed evenly again.

Which load balancing solution you need depends largely on the situation, but if the situation is such that you can avoid stickiness, you should go with as simple a load balancer as possible.

Sessions

PHP sessions (the data we keep between requests, such as shopping carts or login data) are a tricky feature of PHP when it comes to clustering. On one machine, sessions work just fine, but when there are multiple machines in a cluster, sessions can be a problem. To understand why this is, we first need to understand how sessions in PHP work.

Because a session contains the data we want to keep between requests, PHP serializes the data and stores it to a local file. When a script uses the session, this file is read, un-serialized and the data is available; when the script is finished with the session, it writes the changed data back to the file. This fact that a local file is used is what causes problems in a clustered environment. If a visitor is moved from one server to the next between requests, the session data does not automatically move with him. So if the visitor was logged in on one machine, he's logged out on the next. If he was placing elements in his shopping cart, those get lost between requests.

Luckily, there are a few solutions to solve this problem:

- Instead of a local file, store the session files in a folder that is shared between the servers, for example using NFS. This is a viable solution, but causes some overhead. Depending on the number of servers in the cluster, this may or may not be a viable solution.

- PHP has the ability to change the session handler by setting `session.save_handler` in `php.ini` to a different value. With this setting, you can have PHP store its session data in a database instead of on disk. This scales better than NFS, but still can be a bottleneck; If you have 10 servers and a lot of session data, the traffic to the database will be significant. See the documentation for `session.save_handler` for some more details (`http://nl.php.net/manual/en/ref.session.php#ini.session.save-handler`)

- Using this same configuration, you can set the session handler to "memcache" to store the session data in the memcache caching daemon. This is a very high performance way to store the session data in a cluster. If you were already using memcache for output caching, you might as well use it so store sessions.

- We've seen the Zend Platform repeatedly mentioned in this book. And it wouldn't be a true platform if it didn't have a solution for this as well. The Zend Platform (enterprise edition) has a feature called "Session Clustering," which is a solution that shares the session data on the fly between machines. This solution was created with scalability in mind; even with a thousand servers is performs well, because there is no central storage of the session data as in the previous three solutions. Instead, the data is moved around between servers on the fly when users hop from one server to the next.

Using these solutions, sessions can easily be scaled in a clustered environment. Which solution is best, depends on the environment, consider the pros and the cons before you make a decision. If you have trouble deciding on the best strategy, you can always start with one and change to another later on.

Environments

Now that we've defined the hardware infrastructure, we should have a look at the different environments we need. You might expect to need only one environment, but considering this is a book about enterprise grade development, that would not be a good idea. It's a situation most people start with though, but over time, the environment matures. Let's look at the different stages of deployment maturity.

Production Environment

This most basic scenario where there's just a single environment (development is done directly on production), might be suitable for someone's personal blog, but for a serious application or web site, this is seriously not done. Any mistake, or just a change even, can break the production environment. If each step in the maturity of deployment environments had a level, this would be level 0. So let's not waste too many words here, other than that this is a very bad idea, and in general, you should never, ever, touch the production environment directly.

Development and Production Environments

Level 1 is the logical next step. Development is done on a development server and finished products run on the production environment. For single developer projects, this is a very suitable situation, as testing can be done on the development environment. For multi-developer projects, it is useful to have a separate testing environment, as you need a place to test a current development snapshot while development continues. This leads us to the next level up the maturity ladder.

Development, Test and Production

Every developer has his own development environment at level 2. There is one test environment where integration testing is done, or where a QA team tests the software. By doing this in a separate environment, the tests are not affected by continued development by the rest of the developers. So far, we haven't involved the customer yet in the testing efforts; if this is done, it usually happens on production. This means that if the customer reports a bug, it's already in production. So we need to improve the environments some more.

Development, Test, Acceptance and Production

Level 3 introduces the "acceptance" environment for acceptance tests. When a release is done to the customer, this is first installed on this environment, so the customer can test it before it goes into production. If the customer accepts the release, the exact same version is deployed to production. Level 3 is the most common scenario in enterprise PHP projects and suitable for most projects.

Development, Test, Acceptance, Production and Debug

In really large projects, you can run into another issue, even at level 3. What if the team is working on version 2 of the software, while version 1.2 is currently being tested by the customer on the acceptance environment, and all of a sudden something breaks on the production environment. Where do you debug this? You can't debug it on the test environment, because they're working on version 2 there (and even if you could, the customer doesn't usually have access to the test environment). You can't deploy it to acceptance either because the customer is still testing 1.2 and 1.2 isn't ready for production just yet. You could fix it directly on live but that would be risky.

A possible solution in this case is to have a 'debug' environment. It's an exact copy of the production environment (preferably kept in sync automatically). A bug in the live environment can be easily reproduced on the debug environment, fixed, tested, and rolled into production.

This scenario, let's call it "level 4," contains everything you need for your deployment needs. Please note however that the more environments you have, the bigger the overhead of maintaining them. Not all projects require a level 4 environment, so pick one that suits your project.

One final remark on environments: an 'environment' does not necessarily mean a completely separate set of hardware; using virtualization you can run all of them on a single physical server; even without virtualization, some environments, like test and acceptance or production and debug can often be deployed to separate directories and different virtual hosts on the same server.

Deployment Methods

Deployment of a PHP application to an environment can be done in a number of ways.

Manual

The most basic way to deploy an application is to manually upload it to its environment. This can be done using (s)FTP, SCP or whichever the server supports. After uploading the files for the application, you need to create the database, set any directory or file permissions the application needs (e.g. an uploads/ directory that should be writable by the web server).

Source Control

If you are using a source control system such as SVN, an update is fairly easy. The best way is to tag the version that you want to deploy, then checkout the files based on this tag. For an update of the sources, the same routine applies. For this to work, you need to have shell access to the environment and a client for your source control system. On shared hosting environments this can be problematic, but for most dedicated servers this should pose no problem.

Depending on the source control system used, you may or may not have to apply relevant file system permissions after deploying the application. Some source control systems do that for you, others just put the files in place and leave the permissions up to you.

Scripted Release

For larger systems, especially when there are a lot of manual operations going on after the deployment (like setting permissions, updating the database etc.), it's wise to create a deployment script that takes care of these things. Not only does this save time, it will also make it easier for others to perform an install or an update. It also reduces the chance of errors because the script, unlike human beings, can't forget steps or do them differently than previous times.

Installer

The "nicest" way of deploying an application or an update is using a dedicated installer. An installer, which can be a command line program but usually is a web-based application, can take you through all the steps needed to install an application. For most projects the extra effort to create an installer would be overkill, but if the project is an application that will be installed many times, by many different customers or many different users, then an installer is well worth it, because it reduces the support load of supporting users that have trouble deploying the application. This makes installers very suitable for ISV type companies (software vendors).

Migration

For updates of existing applications, regardless of the deployment method, the safest way is to create a new directory, deploy the new application, and then switch directories. If for example your directory is called www, then you could create a www-new and install the app there. If all is well, rename www to www-old and www-new to www, and the application is live. One of the main reasons for doing this instead of copying the files over to the new directories, is that any files you have removed in the new version may remain if you don't remove them in the target directory. Just copying the new version will not remove those files.

We've currently only looked at deployment of the application as a set of source code files. However, there's a little more to an application, and especially when upgrading from one version to the next, this could get us into trouble. I'm talking about the database, the content in the database and file content. File content is the files that users upload through a web application. Sometimes this is stored in the database, so it can be treated like database content, but more often, this is stored directly on disk, and can't easily be versioned because our application users do not have access to the source control system.

Database Structure

The database schema will change from one version to the next. Columns will be added or dropped, entire tables will change, etc. If we deploy new versions of the application's source code, we also need to update the database. This can be done manually but that is not recommended. Especially if you have multiple developers and multiple environments, manual database changes are cumbersome and can easily lead to mistakes if an update is forgotten.

The easiest way to deal with database migration is to work with patch files. A patch file may look like this:

```
-- patch 34
ALTER TABLE customer ADD address2 VARCHAR(200);
```

Every time you commit a set of changes to the repository that requires a database change, include a patch file with the necessary changes. This way, other developers updating their sandboxes can apply the patch to their database (if each developer has its own database, which I do recommend). When a release rolls into the test environment or the production environment, all the patch files can be applied, in the correct order.

There are several patch file strategies. One is to have a single set of patch files for the entire application, another is to have separate patch files per module or component.

Do keep track of the current patch level of a database, use a small table that contains the latest applied patch level for each module. This way, patching the database can easily be scripted; a script can look at the current patch level and apply all available patches in the correct order. When it's done, it updates the patch levels in the database so the next time you run it, the patches aren't executed a second time.

> **i** Note: Always create a backup before patching the database, so you can roll back if something fails.

Please note that in order to update the database, you will have to take it offline for a short period of time. If that is not acceptable, do the same as with files: patch a copy of the database and make that the new live database when done. Be careful with that though; in the meantime data may have been written to the old database; either set the database to read-only, or prepare a script that syncs the content between the databases so you can migrate smoothly.

Database Content

Database patches that change the structure of the database, are responsible for manipulating the data accordingly. For example, if a field moves from one table to the other, the patch file should assume that there is existing data in the table that should not get lost and should be transferred to the new table.

Occasionally, it's not just the structure that changes between versions. There may be some new content that should be placed in the database. The content in the database (the actual data) is hard to version or to put in patch files; you can't write patch files for every new record that one of the users adds. While this could be automated, it's simply not practical.

However, in the cases where you may need to pass content around between environments, you have a few options:

- Database dumps. Development and test databases should operate on data that resembles a real scenario. This can easily be done by occasionally dumping the data from the live environment into an SQL dump file and installing that on the other environments. Using the patch files, this database is then modified in structure so it reflects the current development database schema. Also, the content can then be converted to the new version using the patch files.

- Partial dumps. If a new feature required a new table which should be filled with some initial content, you can dump the contents of that table as a set of

SQL insert statements that can be included in a patch file. This way, small sets of content can easily be rolled into other environments using the already in place patch system.

File Content

A challenging problem is that of file content. For example, images or other files that users upload on a web site. When dumping a database and transferring the content from one environment to the other, you will have references to these uploaded files that do not automatically exist on the other environment. There are a few solutions to this challenge.

- One school of thought is: this type of files is content, hence it should be in the database. If for performance reasons this is not practical, use a caching system, but keep the original content in the database. This way, it can be treated just like other content.

- Version the files. Periodically, sync the files to the source control repository, so that they are versioned just like source files. This is harder than it looks, because you need to take into account that people may remove files, and you have to detect that and remove the file from the source control repository too; otherwise, upon an update, the files that were removed reappear.

- Isolate the files. By isolating all files that are not versioned and not in the database, into a separate subdirectory, you can keep that directory in sync between environments by moving the entire directory around. Using the `rsync` utility, this can even be automated.

All of these methods have advantages and, unfortunately, also disadvantages. There is no "holy grail" yet for dealing with this issue, and as PHP applications grow and become more mature, people will eventually find the best practice way to deal with this. Until then, use the above methods and decide which one works best for your particular situation.

Deployment and Release Profile

In this chapter we have seen ways to handle the deployment of applications and web sites. Deployment is not trivial; by sticking to the procedures outlined in this chapter you can reduce the chance of errors and the amount of time needed for deploying an application or updating it to a new version. Because of the many aspects involved with deployment of new applications or updates, I recommend documenting how the deployment of a particular project is done in a so- *Deployment and Release Profile* (DRP).

This document should at least answer the following questions:

- Which environments are available, and how can they be accessed / where are they located?

- How is source control handled (in terms of tags and branches)?

- What is the procedure for updating an environment to a new version?

- Who is responsible for what?

The document should not only define the technical steps but also the procedures surrounding it; for example, when updating the live environment, the customer needs to be informed, there may be some scheduled down-time; all of this should be documented. For the team, the DRP is useful because it provides a clear overview of how to handle updates to the environment. In the case the regular maintainer of an environment is unavailable, it's not hard for someone else to take over if it's well documented.

For the customer, the DRP provides a clear overview of how updates are handled and it will give him confidence that the team knows what it's doing.

DRPs usually start out as a simple document; sometimes even one page is enough to describe the procedures. Every time you encounter issues or run into a difficult situation, define the solution and add it to the DRP, so the DRP matures as the environment itself matures.

Chapter 14

Implementation

Implementation is often referred to as the entire process from gathering specifications to delivering the application to the client. Since we've already covered many of these steps in separate chapters, in this chapter I refer to implementation as "implementing the application at a client." In other words, helping the (external or internal) customer take the application into production.

Delivery

When the application is finished, you need to deliver it to the customer or end-user. Delivery is not a matter of sending an email with a "Here's your project, have fun" note. There are some things to take into account.

Before an application is taken into production, it's useful to have the customer do a final test to see if everything is acceptable. If the acceptance test uncovers some bugs, you can decide to postpone the release, or to release the product anyway depending on the nature of the bug and available workarounds. A good way to deal with an acceptance test is to define "show stoppers"; these are the bugs that have to be fixed before the site or application can go live. The other issues can be fixed afterward.

Depending on the situation and the customer, you may want to have the customer formally accept the delivery (for example by signing a delivery document). The delivery marks the moment when your support SLA or guarantee period starts. In most situations, if the project has gone well and the delivery has gone smoothly, the delivery is accepted and everything is fine. However, in the occasion the customer doesn't accept the delivery, you could end-up arguing about it for a long period, and the moment at which guarantee or support starts can become fuzzy. When the delivery is not acceptable to the customer, you have a few options:

- Don't deploy the new version to the production environment. Define a new delivery date, define the *acceptance criteria* (what needs to be done in order for the customer to accept the release), fix the issues so they meet the criteria, and retry.

- Agree that the application is accepted, with the exception of a certain set of issues. These issues should then be documented, and you should define a plan of action to fix the issues. In the meantime though, the application is deployed to the production environment.

Whatever the issue, communication is key. If you have a good relationship with your customer, you will be able to work things out. I sometimes encounter development teams who see the customer as "the enemy" and treat a project as a war they want to win. This is not the most fruitful attitude; it's better to consider the customer a partner in the project. The development team and the customer together define the outcome of the project.

Some general advice on delivery:

- Don't do a delivery on Friday; when there is a problem with the new system, it's harder to solve it during the weekend.

- Don't do a delivery during peak traffic. Do it early in the morning when there aren't many visitors (if the application allows it), so you can gradually increase the load and see if the system handles it. Of course, if you did proper performance testing, this should not lead to any surprises.

- Make sure you always have a back-up plan. If something goes wrong, you should have the ability to revert the release (e.g. deploy the previous version of a site or application).

Documentation

A public web site should work without any user documentation, because you can't force a visitor to read the documentation first before he starts using the site. For business applications, this is different. People need to work with the application in a productive way, and applications can be complex. Of course you have done everything in your power to make it as intuitive as possible, but business processes are not trivial and hence applications can sometimes be difficult.

If this is the case, it's important to have proper documentation. Preferably the documentation is provided online to be used from inside the application. This type of documentation is useful to explain screens, options, buttons and other features. "What does this do?", "What should I enter in that field?" are types of questions best answered with help that is only a mouse-click away.

Offline documentation has a different goal. It needs to instruct the user how to work with the system, how to do the things that he needs to do to be productive with it. Instead of "feature based" documentation that describes how the features of a system work, I am in favor of what I call a "task based" manual. In such a task based manual you describe the tasks that the users of the system need to perform from the user's perspective, and what he needs to do to accomplish that task. A task could be "processing an order", or "billing the client". The task then describes how this process is done in the system, explaining which screens to use and which features, in what order, and so forth.

User Training

It may be necessary to provide user training on top of user documentation. Depending on the size of the user base, it may be a good idea to split the group into different roles. This way, you can teach each group of users to perform the tasks that are relevant for them. For example, if you have developed a project management solution, the project managers have different tasks than the project team members, and the board of directors has a different set of tasks too. Since they will be using different parts of the system, they will benefit from a specific training course. The best courses for user training are those that learn by doing. Instead of explaining all the buttons and links in the system, take them through the tasks that they need to perform, by having them actually perform the tasks.

Of course, the level of training and the amount of training required differs per project, per customer, per user etc. Talk to the customer and create a training plan that fits their needs. This could range from a simple one hour presentation to a five day course.

User Feedback

An important thing to deal with when implementing a solution, is feedback from the user. I'm not talking about feedback such as bug reports or change requests, we will deal with that in the Operations and Maintenance chapters. I'm talking about the way the new users or visitors are dealing with the new system; when a new system is implemented, users are going to have to get used to it. This will not always go smoothly.

Even if things are better, some users will complain that it's "different." Sometimes this is hard to understand, and it can even be frustrating. You've worked hard to deliver a fancy new system that meets the requirements and that works flawlessly, but still, the users aren't as enthusiastic as you had expected. Of course there can be specific reasons, such as things that are wrong ("flawless" doesn't exist in software development) or that do not match the expectations. If that is the case, then these problems are solvable. But often, there are no specific reasons. This situation is easier to deal with if you understand where this comes from.

Imagine your application is like a new pair of jeans. Your favorite jeans are completely worn out and you have to buy a new pair. The new jeans are never as comfy as the old ones; they look different, they feel different. But after a while, the new jeans grow on you and you start to like them, and before you know it, they are your new favorite jeans.

So, to deal with "acceptance" we just have to help the users get comfortable in the new jeans. Show them how they can do the things they used to do, but in a different way. Try to show them how the new way is better, and before you know it, your system is their new pair of favorite jeans.

Marketing

So far we've looked at implementation issues for web applications or sites that deal with existing users. For web sites that are completely fresh however, things are different. There are no users to educate and no people to help adapt to a new situation. For fresh sites, the implementation consists mostly of getting visitors. This is a matter of (e-)marketing. Marketing is so wildly different from running a PHP development project that my only advice is to get someone in who is familiar with it, or to outsource it to a marketing agency. Also, this is something that the development team is not often involved in. If you work for a customer, this is work for the customer.

However, if you are a development team and you built a web site on your own, there are a few small pieces of advice I can give you to get you started.

- Viral marketing is popular. Generating buzz around a web site and using an invitation system to get new users, who can in their turn, invite other users, has two effects: it makes sure that you grow steadily and it makes people curious after your service. The most extreme example of this type of marketing was Google's Gmail; they were "invite only" for many months after their initial launch. In the end however, almost anybody had an account, because everybody knew somebody who knew somebody who had an account. If done properly, growth can be exponential.

- Get some free press. Blog about the site, and make sure that others talk about it too. For Web 2.0 sites, there are a few web sites you can get a free review or listing, and that immediately gets you traffic. These are sites like The Museum of Modern Betas (`http://momb.socio-kybernetics.net/`), TechCrunch (`http://www.techcrunch.com/`) or Emily Chang (`http://www.emilychang.com/`).

- Run ad campaigns on Google and/or Yahoo; this is easy enough even for a non-marketeer to work with (although marketeers tend to do a lot better job in picking the right keywords, the right campaigns etc.), and you define your own budget.

These basic tips get you a small number of users to start off with. If the new site is good; people will talk about it and news will spread. If you need a bigger launch and want to go for the big numbers from the start, you need to launch a true marketing campaign with professional help. One word of caution; they say "you never get a second chance to make a first impression." This is true for web sites as well. If your service is not good, the quality is low or the functionality is not what your users want, you will have negative publicity, and it's really hard to make up for that. So prepare carefully.

Evaluation

When the whole solution is implemented in the production environment, there's one more useful thing to do. Evaluate the entire project with the customer, to check what they think was good, or what has room for improvement. Constantly evaluating each project will help you improve your own processes and do the next project even better than the previous one. This "continuous improvement" will make projects more efficient and increase quality.

It's also a good idea to do a team evaluation; everybody will have encountered issues during the project and everybody will have some idea of what went well and what could be improved. Discussing these points and thinking of areas of improvement for the next project, will increase the maturity of the development team.

Chapter 15

Operations

The "operations" phase of a project starts directly after a web site or application goes live for the first time. Many development teams think this is the point where the project ends. We celebrate with a glass of champagne, or, depending on the geek-factor of the development team, with the same pizza and coke used throughout the development of the project, only this time with extra anchovies.

If your team is responsible for maintaining the application, enjoy the launch festivities, as the project now moves into a new phase with different challenges. "Operations" translates freely to "keeping the site up and running." Making changes to the application is a different story, which I will cover in the next chapter.

Monitoring

Keeping a site up and running is hard if you don't know the status of the site. Monitoring is key. If you don't monitor, things may break, and this may go unnoticed for a while. With business applications you'll get feedback from users relatively soon, but with public web sites, feedback is much more uncommon. For every user that reports broken functionality, maybe a 1000 users will have noticed the problem but just moved on, went to the site of a competitor or the next item in their search results. Problems can result in a decrease in the number of visitors, and worse, in the case the application or web site is revenue generating, can cost money.

In the chapter on Deployment we learned that you shouldn't touch code on a live environment. If we abide by that rule, all is well and monitoring is not necessary, right? Wrong; there are many things that can break a site, even when not touching the code. Users with access to the back-end of a web site may break things, hardware may break down, operating system updates may wreak havoc, sudden spikes in traffic might bring the site down. So no matter how solid your deployment is, you still need to monitor.

There are many things that can be monitored; let's look at some of the most important ones.

Infrastructure

Hardware is fragile. Hard disks still have tiny moving parts, and the more traffic a site generates, the more the parts move, and the more likely something will break at some point. Even if the system has a RAID configuration that covers a failing disk, there's still a chance that things break (I've once seen a large site go down unexpectedly because 3 out of 5 disks in a disk array almost simultaneously thought "I've had enough, put your bits somewhere else" and refused service).

So it's important to monitor disk condition. It's also important to monitor disk space. If a server runs out of disk space, bad things can happen. Other things to monitor include memory status, CPU temperature and network status. It's best to monitor all parts of the infrastructure that can break. A popular tool for keeping an eye on infrastructure is Nagios, a free and open source monitoring tool for Linux and Unix environments (`http://www.nagios.org/`)

There is also a wide variety of commercial monitoring tools available.

Functionality

It's good to keep an eye on the functionality of an application and check if it still works. This can be done by periodically running automated tests, and/or with some scripts that perform some basic content checks. For example, you may retrieve the contents of a few important pages of the web site and check if certain content elements are present on the page.

Another indicator that functionality might be broken are the entries in the PHP error log file. If you have turned on PHP error logging, keep an eye on the log. Unexpected error messages or a sudden increase of certain messages might indicate a problem in the application.

Zend has created a product to monitor PHP applications and to channel errors to the right person in a development team. You might call it an "application server for PHP." It goes further than logging and helps find the cause of problems in PHP scripts. Information can be found at `http://www.zend.com/en/products/platform`.

If you want users to report functional problems, be sure to incorporate a form for them to provide feedback. If it's easy to provide feedback, the chance that a user will report a problem increases dramatically.

Statistics

Track user statistics and check for anomalies. If the number of visitors a day suddenly drops, something may be wrong. If the average number of pages a visitor views drops, that might also indicate a problem somewhere. Statistics are not only useful to detect problems, but also to spot places where the web site can be improved.

I find Google Analytics a useful tool to track statistics for PHP web sites. It takes dynamic URLs into account, and it allows you to define "funnels." A funnel represents the steps that a user takes before he reaches a "goal" on the web site (for example, completing an order). In each step, a certain percentage of visitors will leave, e.g., when 100 visitors visit the homepage, 70 of them will click on the "products" page, 50 will actually view a product, 20 will place an order, 10 will complete checkout. By monitoring the "conversion rate" statistics, you can track functional problems: each problem that occurs within the funnel, will lead to a lower percentage reaching the next step, hence a lower percentage generating revenue. Google Analytics can be found at `http://www.google.com/analytics/`.

Performance

Performance is an important thing to monitor. Because performance issues can have impact on the entire server, it is important to signal performance issues as soon as possible. (Dips in performance often have a snowball effect; if the site becomes sluggish, people start to hit the "reload" button, causing even more requests and increasing the problem.)

Performance can be measured indirectly by looking at indicators like CPU load, or directly using tools that can measure PHP performance. Also, the Zend Platform that was mentioned above has several monitoring techniques to measure the performance of scripts and queries.

Revenue

For commercial web sites it is important to keep an eye on the performance of a web site in terms of revenue. Even if technically everything is going fine, there could be functional or content problems that may cause the regular flow to be interrupted. In the case of web shops, you can track the amount of orders over time, for hotel web sites you can measure the number of reservations, or the average turnover per hour. This way you can detect anomalies. For example, if your web-shop generally has a turnover of 1 000 dollars an hour, and all of a sudden this drops to 0 for no apparent reason, you will want to investigate what is causing this.

A complicating factor is that turnover on commercial web sites is often dependent on the time of day, the day of the week or even the day of the month (for example, office supply stores will sell more during office hours, while holidays will be sold more during the weekend. A really thorough monitoring solution should take these variations into account. For example, you can monitor the normal flow for a while and keep track of an average turnover in a database. Then, the monitoring script can measure the turnover in the last hour (or in the last 5 minutes, depending on how fine-grained you want the monitoring to be) and compare that to a value that is stored in the database.

It is important to measure this, because if you don't notice a problem until it's already too late, you will incur revenue loss.

Growth

Monitoring of the items mentioned in this chapter can be used not only to detect problems, but also to measure the growth of a web site. By tracking the indicators, you can see if a web site grows according to plan. This is an important measurement, from a commercial point of view, but also helps detect when it is time to invest in new hardware or when to start optimizing a web site.

Preventive Maintenance

An important task in the operation of an application or web site is maintenance to prevent problems. Monitoring is great to notice when things go wrong, but there are some things we can do to prevent problems from happening.

Security Updates

There is a lot of software involved when running a web site or web-application. The code itself is, in comparison, just a small part. Other software includes PHP, PHP extensions, any frameworks or libraries used in the project, a web server, a database, an operating system and utility programs. Each of these are vulnerable to security issues. Hackers and script-kiddies are constantly on the look-out for such issues. If a vulnerability is discovered in a software component, they look for sites using these components and will try to exploit them. Therefore, it is important to keep track of these issues and take measures when a vulnerability is discovered.

For many software components and programs you can subscribe to a mailing-list where security announcements are posted. Some post this on their web site, so it's also important to keep an eye on the web site of components that are used. There are also some generic web sites that publish security vulnerabilities in public software components. Usually, these sites only disclose the information once a fix is provided by the author of the software, so you can immediately update the software if a vulnerability has been announced. The following web sites are useful to keep track of security vulnerabilities :

- SecurityFocus (`http://www.securityfocus.com/vulnerabilities`); this site lists vulnerabilities in open source and closed source products. It also hosts the popular "bugtraq" mailing-list, which is a well-known mailing-list that publishes security vulnerabilities)

- The Open Source Vulnerability Database (OSVDB) (`http://osvdb.org`); this site focuses on vulnerabilities in Open Source projects.

Bug Fixes

Slightly less important than security fixes, but still important, are fixes for bugs. Most bug fixes are functionality bugs, and if you're not affected by them, updating a software component is not necessary (and not wise; if it's not broken for you, don't fix it). However, sometimes bug fixes can be important; if a vendor discovers that certain situations can lead to data corruption or crashes it is wise to do a preventive update of that software component. Keep the Quality Assurance chapter in mind: if you are forced to upgrade a component, test the application thoroughly as each upgrade of a component in the system might cause incompatibilities and can introduce new bugs.

Log Rotation

In the beginning of this chapter we discussed logging; if you add logging, be sure to configure it in such a way that log files are rotated (in other words, a new log-file is created after a certain amount of time, usually daily), and the oldest log files are cleaned up or archived. This may not seem important, but in a running system, if log files just keep on growing and growing, eventually they will take up all disk space. Everybody who has set-up a system with standard logging has at some point run into the problem that disks were full because the log files were huge. You can prevent this situation by implementing log rotation from the start.

Operational Plan

Monitoring is good, but if nothing happens when something bad occurs, it's pretty useless. To make sure that the right action is taken, define an operational plan. In an operational plan you write down:

- Common things that may go wrong. Some things are predictable and easy to document. Others you may need to add once they happened so they are documented for the next time.

- Common solutions to common problems. This can be as simple as instructions for restarting the web server, or more complex with instructions on where to look to find the cause of a problem.

- A quick reference; a quick overview of the system, or pointers to the system documentation.

- What actions should be taken when something happens (notification of customers, investigating and solving the problem).

- Responsibilities; who is responsible for fixing what type of problem, which third parties are responsible for certain components.

- A contact list; who should be contacted, when and how.

- An escalation scheme. If the problem persists and can not be solved by the documentation, what to do next? For example, bring in a senior, restart the environment, etc.

When bad things happen, adrenaline will often interfere with common sense and clear reasoning. Having an operational plan with a clear set of instructions on what to do, will help to keep a grip on any bad situation.

Chapter 16

Maintenance

Once operational, a project is likely to require maintenance. In the previous chapter we looked at monitoring. Sometimes monitoring reveals a problem in the software which needs to be fixed. We will look at troubleshooting the application later in this chapter. Firstly though we will look at a different type of change. Software is never finished, and changing conditions or changing insights will require changes to the software. We'll look first at some aspects of managing these changes.

Change Management

When a project team is still young, changes are often dealt with on an ad hoc basis. The customer calls in with a request, the developer writes some code which gets deployed to the production environment and the customer is happy. For a while, this will seem like a good idea. But eventually, such an "adhocracy" will run into several problems:

- The quality of the software degrades. Because all new changes are put on top of existing code, one after the other, the existing architecture of the application starts to erode.

- With each change, the maintainability of the application gets worse, as it's no longer clear what goes where.

- The project team will have moved on, and no longer has time for changes. This is more a planning issue than a technical issue, but we'll look at this aspect later on in this chapter.

- The line between support issues and new features is sometimes blurry; when dealing with changes ad-hoc, it is unclear what time is spent on behalf of the customer, and what should or should not be billed.

To avoid problems like this, we have to structure the way we deal with changes. There are a few things we can do to define a structure that will help us organize changes.

Administration

Keep track of all change requests in an issue tracker, so the status of the request can be properly monitored. This not only provides a single source of information for the developer, the customer and the project manager, it will also be useful when monitoring how many changes a customer requests. If the frequency of change requests is high, you may want to offer the customer a "version 2" of the software.

Developing the Change

Treat every change as a mini-project; this means first defining what the customer actually needs (which, like we discussed earlier during the requirements phase, is not always what the customers asks), then designing the solution, adjusting the functional and technical design, implementing the change, testing it and deploying it. Essentially, it's most of what we've seen in this book so far, but on a smaller scale. This may seem like overhead, but it's just a more structured approach; in the long term it will save time and keep the quality of the software at a higher level.

Documentation

Keep technical documentation up to date; this will help with future changes. In the code, you can refer to the issue in the issue tracker so you can always read why certain things were changed. If you look at the code in the future and can no longer remember making the changes, you can still read why the code is written the way it is.

Troubleshooting

Change requests from the customer are not the only reason to change the software. Sometimes bugs are encountered which need to be fixed. The important aspects of bug-fixing have been discussed throughout this book in various chapters. An important chapter in this respect is the Quality Assurance chapter, to make sure that your bug-fixes are of the right quality. Another is the Deployment chapter, where we covered how to roll out fixes into a production environment. And in the Tools chapter, we had a look at debugging and root-cause analysis, two important tools that help you locate a bug.

What makes troubleshooting different from the initial programming, or the fixes during the testing phase, is the fact that troubleshooting can happen long after the project has been finished. This makes it more difficult, because the development team has since taken on other assignments, and knowledge about the project where troubleshooting is required may have been diminished. This is why it's important to keep documentation up to date, so you can review the information you need to fix the bug. Documentation was covered in various chapters throughout the book. Troubleshooting also encompasses fixing performance problems. In the optimization chapter, we have looked at various ways to find a performance problem, and how to fix it.

It's not a coincidence that the troubleshooting section refers to topics we have already discussed earlier in the book. Everything we have seen so far is intended to make life easier, to increase the quality of software and to make the software more maintainable.

Planning

An often-heard problem in development teams is that troubleshooting and maintenance of existing applications is problematic with regards to planning. You're working on a new project, but an issue from an older project comes up. This requires a context switch from one project to the other and cuts into the schedule of the new project. The best way to mitigate this is to minimize maintenance. This book should have given you enough information to increase the quality of your development lifecycle, and you will notice that following the ways described in this book will decrease the amount of time you need to spend on maintenance. Still, maintenance can never be completely eliminated. There are a few workable solutions for the problem of troubleshooting older projects when you're working on new projects. Which ones are viable depends on the size of your organization and the situation.

Reserve Time

Dedicate time for older projects; based on experience you should be able to estimate how much time is spent on maintenance for these projects. Reserving space in the project schedule accordingly will not endanger new projects.

Service Level Agreements

Negotiate a Service-Level Agreement (SLA) with the customer that covers troubleshooting of a live environment; this way, the time reserved for troubleshooting can be governed by an SLA to cover the cost. An SLA can also define response times so you can design a structured way of dealing with problems in existing applications.

Service Team

If the number of existing projects requiring maintenance is significant, it might be worthwhile to create a dedicated team. If a project is properly documented, it's fairly easy to transfer maintenance to a different group of developers. Such a dedicated maintenance team has more time for the customer, and more time to solve the problem.

Being part of such a "service team" may not sound attractive to many developers, but some developers will like the fact that they are working on challenging problems and a wide variety of applications, sites or customers. They essentially run projects too, but of a much smaller timeframe.

A service team dedicated to application maintenance is also a good way to educate junior developers. They get to know your customers, your projects, your products, and see a lot of existing code, so they can become more familiar with your coding guidelines and coding style. A few words of caution: if the service team is dealing with bugs only, the team members will see only code that is wrong, has flaws or is of less quality in general. Having the team work not only on bugs but also on new/changed features will prevent this. Also, if the team only consists of junior developers, they will lack guidance and the quality of service can be sub-optimal. If you create a service team, use a mix of junior and senior developers.

Part III

The Big Picture

Chapter 17

Development Methodologies

Requirements, architecture, development, testing and the rest of the topics covered in this book, were covered each as a separate chapter. But together, they form a complete Software Development Life Cycle. The order in which I wrote the chapters seems logical, but this doesn't mean we always execute them in this order. In this chapter I cover some 'development methodologies'. These are guiding principles that define how the life cycle is structured.

Waterfall

The 'classic' software methodology is the so-called waterfall model. This model is very structured. It defines that we perform the steps in a predefined order and only in that order.

Figure 17.1

The advantage of the waterfall model is that we exactly know what we are doing and when we are doing it. The big problem however is that the process, like a real world waterfall, is one-way. It has no way of coping with changing insights or changing requirements, and requires us to know exactly what we are going to build.

For some projects this is a useful methodology. For many projects however this is problematic. Customers often do not know exactly what they want, and during the project, requirements may change. In particular in Internet projects, because the Internet changes so rapidly, changing requirements are something to take into account, but the waterfall model does not offer any possibility to do this.

Still, the waterfall model is widely used and often taught in computer science institutes. I have encountered customers that insisted on the waterfall model, convincing the development team that the requirements were clear and would not change, and more often than not, eventually they did change. It would be a career-limiting move to tell the customer "I told you so," so take this into account when applying the waterfall model.

Nobody has a crystal ball that predicts the outcome of a project, especially in big projects which span multiple man-months. This is why projects often miss their deadline and run severely over budget. The waterfall methodology requires that you can foresee everything when you're in the first phase of the project. IT history has proven that this is almost never possible.

Rapid Application Development

The opposite of the 'crystal ball' approach of the waterfall model is a methodology that assumes that nothing is certain and everything can change. *Rapid Application Development* (or RAD) is a methodology where the team works from a set of initial requirements, but develops the application using prototypes.

First, a simple prototype is built that implements some of the requirements, and this prototype is discussed with the customer. Based on the prototype and the feedback, a second prototype is built. This process continues until the customer is happy and no feedback remains.

The advantage of this approach is that a project is developed in close cooperation with the customer. A disadvantage is that this approach tends to focus on the superficial; the things that the customer can see. Architecture, performance and other "invisible" aspects are less important. This is why many RAD development environments such as Visual Basic or Delphi focus on "what you see is what you get" editors to build screens.

This focus sometimes leads to misunderstanding between the development team and the customer ("You showed me this screen three weeks ago, why does it take three weeks to finish it?"). The fact that the underlying business logic is often more complex than what the customer sees on the screen is sometimes difficult to explain.

I find RAD useful for small projects, where an application is merely a set of simple screens without much business logic or architectural complexity. For bigger projects, I would not recommend the RAD approach.

Agile

Unhappy with the result of the traditional methodologies, a group of 17 experts in the field of software development wrote a manifesto that called for better ways to develop software. *The Agile Manifesto* (`http://agilemanifesto.org/`) centers around the following basic principles:

- People are more important than tools

- Working software is more important than comprehensive documentation

- The customer is part of the project

- Changes are inevitable

"Agile development" is not a methodology in itself; there are many methodologies that are considered to be agile. A methodology can call itself "agile" when it adheres to the principles from the manifesto.

Iterations

An important aspect of agile development methodologies is the iterative approach to development. The development life-cycle is broken down into small iterations of a predefined size, each of which is a development process on its own. During each iteration, a set of requirements is implemented. First the design is adjusted to accommodate the new requirements, then the source is refactored to add the new functionality, the software is tested and presented to the customer. Each iteration ends with a working system.

At the start of an iteration, the list of requirements to be built is discussed with the customer. If there are new or changed requirements, these can be taken into account as well. Because the iterations are small, typically no more than a few weeks, it is ideal for Test Driven Development. For each feature test cases are written; they guarantee that in later iterations, despite the refactoring that will be done on the source code, the existing functionality isn't broken.

Budgets

An argument to use the waterfall model instead of an agile approach is that in the waterfall model is fixed, so you know what you get, what it costs and when you will get it, whereas in an agile process, since change is factored in (each iteration the customer can adjust the goals), you have less certainties. In practice however, this is usually the other way round. Because in a waterfall project things can happen that were unforeseen when the project started, and changes can't be taken into account, a waterfall project often misses its deadline and goes over budget. Agile projects on the other hand offer a better ability to steer on budgets. Because iterations are fixed size, and you can define a number of iterations up front, you are in control of the budget. If changes occur or things do not go the way they seem, you can take measures for the following iteration to get the project back on track. For example, if the customer has a fixed budget but changes his mind about a certain feature, you can discuss the impact with him and perhaps drop a less important requirement in favor of the new one. Because contact with the customer is much more frequent in an Agile process, there's more opportunity to steer the project towards a successful end result.

Continuous Improvement

Iterations are useful to apply continuous improvement. If you start an iteration with an evaluation of the previous one, you can immediately improve the process for the next iteration. This way, the project can be kept on track more easily. In the traditional model, where the customer would only get to see the end result at the end of the project, evaluations are usually done at the end. This is useful for the next project, but for the current project, it's already too late. Doing the evaluation per iteration will improve the project while it's underway, which typically leads to an end result that is more satisfactory to the customer and with less stress for the development team.

Examples of Agile methodologies

I mentioned that agile is not a methodology in itself, but a set of methodologies following *The Agile Manifesto*. Here are some examples of agile methodologies. If you would like to apply an agile methodology, I would recommend you investigate the differences between the methodologies mentioned here, and buy a good book on the methodology of choice, or to get some training.

- Extreme Programming (XP). Key aspects of XP are: Test Driven Development, collective ownership of the code, Pair Programming and Continuous Integration. Some of the elements of XP are controversial; their result is questionable. Most projects employing XP use only the parts they feel are right for their project. This is okay, XP defines that you should only use those aspects which help your project.

- Scrum. The Scrum methodology is different from XP but still agile. In a Scrum project, a ScrumMaster is assigned, who is responsible for maintaining the Scrum process and removing barriers. Iterations in Scrum are called 'sprints'. A 'product owner' is defined who is responsible for defining what features get implemented in a sprint. Scrum also has some practical guidelines for certain activities; for example for Scrum meetings, it defines some rules (such as the requirement that everybody stands during the meeting) to keep the meetings short and on topic.

XP and Scrum are the two most well known agile methodologies. Both have some strong points and some controversial aspects. In practice, it's possible to use a combination of the two, where a project team applies those aspects of the two methodologies they find practical for the project.

ITIL

The Information Technology Infrastructure Library (ITIL) is not strictly a development methodology, but it's closely related, so this chapter is a good one to discuss it. We have covered not only the pre-production aspects of the development life cycle but also the post-production elements, such as operations, maintenance and change management. Since many of the aspects of these elements are not PHP specific, we can look at how others have solved these issues. ITIL is a vast collection of descriptions of these aspects, all focused on the service that we need to deliver to customers.

Topics covered by ITIL include:

- Incident management

- Setting up a service desk

- Change management

- Service Level Agreements

- Availability management

Although ITIL is huge, it's useful to look at when implementing some of the topics covered in this book. A good starting point is the Wikipedia article on this subject, which can be found at `http://en.wikipedia.org/wiki/ITIL`.

Chapter 18

Project Management

We are near the end of the book. We've covered the entire PHP software development life cycle. There are a few bits left that I want to point out, regarding project management. This isn't a complete "how to do PHP project management" chapter; there is enough literature on project management already that is perfectly applicable to PHP projects. This chapter just contains a few general topics that I have encountered when working with PHP teams and project managers.

Removing Barriers

A project manager deals with most of the topics covered in this book. Not in the sense that the project manager is personally involved in them, but he does have to make sure that things are done properly, in time and within budget. An important way to make a project succeed is to focus on the bottlenecks. On a regular basis, check what the factors are that are slowing down the project and find a way to fix them.

When some developers run into issues with their code, they tend to really dive into the problem until they find a solution. They would rather find out for themselves how to fix something than asking someone else to help them. Sometimes this can unnecessarily slow down a project. For the project manager, it is important to keep in touch with the developers and recognize situations like this. You can't know everything and it's OK to help each other out in a project.

Another way to keep a project on track is to act as a buffer. Development is a complex job at times, and any distraction will cause a "context switch" in the mind of the developer. This means that if a developer is working on a task, and gets interrupted to fix something in a different project, he needs to get into the other project, and when he gets back to his original project, it takes time to get into that again. A project manager can act as a buffer to make sure that people are only distracted when they can handle it (e.g. in between tasks, near the end of the day). One way to do this is to have customers never call the developer directly, but have them call the project manager instead. The project manager can then decide when the development team can handle the call and have the developers call back when possible.

Dealing with Developers

Project managers who have a technical background or who have been a developer in the past, know what it's like to develop software. Often however, project managers have a different, non-technical background, for example in management or communication. Or, as I usually say, they are not hindered by any technical knowledge. This has advantages and disadvantages. The most important part of managing a project is communication, so the main advantage of someone from that area of expertise is that they are well equipped to handle all aspects of communication.

Cal Evans, editor in chief of the Zend Devzone, a popular site for PHP developers, has written an interesting article on how to deal with developers. It's an article from 1999 but still has a lot of relevance. For project managers without a technical background, this is an interesting read about the psyche of the developer and how to deal with it. The article is called *Nerd Herding* and can be found at `http://blog.calevans.com/nerd-herding/`

Sharpening the Saw

If business is going great, everybody is busy all the time, and there's no time left to have a critical look at the organization or the development team. Some things in the process may need to be improved, some tools may need to be enhanced, but there's no time to do it.

There's a common story about a woodworker that is sawing wood with a blunt saw. Because his saw is blunt, he can only saw so many trees and he has to work hard to meet his daily target. Someone sees all the hard work and the blunt saw, steps up to him and asks "You know, if you sharpen this saw, you could saw a lot faster." His response: "Sure, but I have no time, I need to get these trees done by the end of the day." A nice loop: by never sharpening the saw, he never has time to sharpen the saw.

Sometimes you need to accept a short term loss of productivity to sharpen the saw, so that once it's sharp, you're productivity is increased, and you'll recover from the short loss soon, so on the long term, your overall productivity grows. A good way to deal with this problem is to just calculate time in the project plan for sharpening the saw.

Innovation

Sharpening the saw is one thing, but inventing a more efficient saw is even better. When it comes to the tools you use to develop software, this is similar. If you can innovate the products you use, you can make leaps in productivity. For example if you have a CMS that takes you 40 hours to build a site, and you can spend a day to bring that down to 36 hours, that is 8 hours well spent, as in 2 projects you will have return on investment for this innovation.

A non-intrusive, and fun way to innovate is to combine innovation with a reward system. Project managers tend to calculate some buffer when planning a project. If a developer states he can do something in 32 hours, it is likely that he can do it in 28 hours as well, as he will have included a buffer. Working on innovative things is usually fun, and a nice extra stimulus for keeping things within the planned timeframe, is to use the buffer for innovation. If the developer does the job within 28 hours, he can use the remaining 4 hours to work on fun things. If he's late and needs 32 hours, the extra time is used for the project slack. Mind you that the danger is that there may be times that no time is left to do innovation. For product innovation, this is OK. For true sharpening of the saw however, you should actually plan time.

Index